THE KEY OF LOVE

ROBERT AND KATHY KELSEY

iUniverse, Inc.
Bloomington

The Key of Love

Scripture and Bible verses in this book are from Biblesoft's PC Study Bible, Version 4.2B, and the following Bibles: The Message Bible, AMP (Amplified Version), NIV (New International Version), and NAS (New American Standard).

All scripture is from the King James Version of the Bible, unless otherwise noted.

iUniverse books may be ordered through booksellers or by contacting:

iUniverse
1663 Liberty Drive
Bloomington, IN 47403
www.iuniverse.com
1-800-Authors (1-800-288-4677)

ISBN: 978-1-4401-4919-1 (sc)
ISBN: 978-1-4401-4920-7 (ebk)

Printed in the United States of America

iUniverse rev. date: 11/19/2011

AND I WILL GIVE YOU THE KEYS TO THE KINGDOM OF HEAVEN

MATTHEW 16:19

THE KEY OF LOVE

A SPECIAL THANKS

Our special thanks to all of you that have blessed us over these past years, mentoring us and encouraging us to keep doing those things that God has asked us to do, leading and directing us by your words, actions and your examples. Because you kept the faith, that example allowed us to follow in your footsteps and become an example to others.

DEDICATION

This book is dedicated to you the reader that you would know and understand that great love that God has for you.

Our prayer is that God will use this book to bring you to understand that God has you on His mind and wants you to have "the good life" that He has prearranged and made ready for you to live.
(Ephesians 2:10 AMP)

CONTENTS

INTRODUCTION

This book is the result of many years of study and prayer, meditating on the Word, making notes, and assembling those notes into something I believe will be a blessing to others who are seeking God in their lives.

I discovered that God was telling me in Matthew 6:33, to "Seek first of all the Kingdom of God and all of His righteousness." And when I went looking, I wasn't able to find anyone who knew much of anything about what I was asking. So I set out to remedy that situation. And in doing so, I learned early on to have a total dependency upon God to give the answers I was seeking. I had to yield myself to the Holy Spirit who lives in me, because one can not get spiritual answers from the physical. I had to learn to differentiate between the Holy Spirit and the devil talking to me. I had to learn to walk by faith and to step out and obey God. I had to learn, as I read the Word of God, my trust in Him and my faith would grow and go beyond what I could ever ask or think. I learned that my faith would grow by hearing the Word of God over and over again, and that listening is not a onetime thing; I had to keep at it, day after day, week after week, month after month, and year after year until it became a lifestyle. I also learned I could activate that faith by speaking the Word of God over any given situation which would require God to move on my behalf.

I learned that without God's love we have religion, and that church doctrine forms the basis of most people's Christian beliefs. Church doctrine has the power to hold people tight within the fabric of a church, and the belief system of the church is all that many people know. They cannot see beyond it, and they fear looking.

I discovered that religion is a set of rules to be obeyed whereby one hopes to enter into a relationship with God by getting his act together. Christianity is a personal relationship with God where He will accept you just the way you are and change you from the inside out if you will listen to and obey Him.

In James 1:25 we see ". . . whoso looketh into the perfect law of liberty, and continueth therein, he being not a forgetful hearer, but a doer of the work, this man shall be blessed in his deed." The perfect law of liberty is the Word of God. We have to be determined to not be a "forgetful hearer, but a doer of the work," which will result in our being blessed by our deeds. The blessing lies in getting the proper instructions, hearing them, following and doing them, and hanging in there no matter what others think or say.

As a new believer, you are a new creature, a new creation in Christ Jesus living in an old, unresurrected body. You are still in the flesh, with an unsurrendered soul, and a born-again spirit indwelt by the Spirit of God (II Corinthians 5:17). That old nature or your unsurrendered soul will be the root of most of your problems, and it is most important to learn how to deal with it.

As your new spiritual nature begins to grow in you, the trouble will begin. Your old nature will become sharply aware something has suddenly appeared on the scene that could be totally disastrous to the free reign it has held on your life, and it will respond in kind.

God in His infinite wisdom has made provision for us to walk into renewal and restoration right here on this earth while we are still in our mortal bodies. Jesus defeated the devil at Calvary and He has given us the weapons to enforce that victory in our lives. Titus 3:5 (NIV) says, "He saved us, not because of any righteous things we had done, but because of His mercy. He saved us through the washing of rebirth and renewal by the Holy Spirit."

Many people have experienced the new birth in Christ Jesus, but still hold on tightly to their old ways not knowing what God expects of them. They hurt many people because they are ignorant and do not have an understanding of God's love and they are not allowing God's grace to shine in their lives.

We have all received God's covenant rights which He has for His children. These include being able to override Satan and break loose from his bondages. Jesus said in John 14:12, "He that believeth on me, the works that I do shall he do also; and greater works than these shall he do; because I go unto my Father." God has given us an assignment and He has made provision for us to provide us with everything we need to complete the task. We are told in I John 3:8 that Jesus, the Son of God, was manifested, that He might destroy the works of the devil. II Peter 2:2-11 gives us a good overall view of what God will do in your life if only you will give Him a chance.

Such is God's will for your life; but you will have to make the choice to answer the call on your life here on earth, and get yourself into alignment and agreement with God's will in heaven. God will never force you to do anything, but He will help you. Never will God's will take you where His grace will not keep and support you. Philippians 2:13 (AMP) tells us, "[Not in your own strength] for it is God Who is all the while effectually at work in you [energizing and creating in you the power and desire], both to will and to work for His good pleasure and satisfaction and delight."

Any limitations you encounter in your walk with God will be self imposed because nothing is impossible with God because "All things are possible to him that believeth" (Mark 9:23, Luke 1:37).

As you study the Word of God you will become aware it is very offensive to your soul. The old you won't want anything to do with it and you will have to force yourself to yield to the love that God has for you and the works of the Holy Spirit, yield yourself to the wisdom of God, yield to the understanding of God, and yield when you hear revelation knowledge from God. For "Blessed are they which do hunger and thirst after righteousness: for they Shall be filled (Matthew 5:6)." Your desire to know what God has prepared for you can only be revealed to you by a relationship with the Holy Spirit.

What you are about to study is the result of those years of study and fellowship with God. I encourage you to read the last chapter first and receive my prayer for you.

Are you ready to believe God? Are you ready to please God? Are you ready to catch the vision of what God has for you? Are you ready to enter into God's plan for you today? To do so, you must strive to have absolute faith so that you can receive all good things from the divine source of everything. As you build absolute faith through hearing God's Word, you will receive from the divine source of everything, because "every good gift and every perfect gift is from above, and cometh down from the Father of lights, with whom is no variableness, neither shadow of turning" (James 1:17).

Hebrews 11:6 (AMP) tells us ". . . that without faith it is impossible to please and be satisfactory to Him. For whoever would come near to God must [necessarily] believe that God exists and that He is the rewarder of those who earnestly and diligently seek Him [out]." Do you want God to reward you? Obtaining great faith is as easy as feeding your spirit as often as you feed your body. Matthew 4:4 tells us that what bread or food is to the body, the Word of God is to the spirit, or the heart of man. So, just as you can feed your body, you can feed your faith, because God's Word is faith food.

My object in this lesson is to get across the point that "the Son of man came to save that which was lost" and bring them into a relationship with the Father just like Adam experienced before the fall. He has made provision for us to walk into renewal and restoration right here on the earth while we are still in our mortal bodies (Matthew 18:11; John 3:17, 10:10; Titus 3:5).

This book is designed to be a study guide to get you from where you are to where God wants you to be. Have your Bible with you as you read. Take the time to look up and study the numerous references to scripture herein, as well as cross-references, which appear in parentheses following many of the Bible quotations.

I want you to experience a closer walk with God—to know Him and understand just how much He loves and cares for you. Ask the Holy Spirit to help you as you study. He is here to help you and guide you into all truth (John 16:7, 13). Look up each scripture, read several verses before and after the noted verse and study it out, meditate on it, and let the Word of God be your final judge. God has sent the Holy Spirit into your life to guide you into all truth (John 16:13, I Thessalonians 5:21). So take full advantage of all that God has provided for you to make your life all God has created you to be.

1

THE KEYS TO THE KINGDOM OF HEAVEN

> . . . And I will give unto thee the keys to the kingdom of
> Heaven; and whatever you bind (declare to be improper
> and unlawful) on earth must be what is already bound in
> heaven; and whatever you loose (declare lawful) on earth
> must be what is already loosed in heaven (Matthew 16:19,
> 18:18 AMP).

A key, from the Greek word *kleis*, "a key" is used to mean; knowledge of
the revealed will of God, by which men enter into the life that pleases God.

With these keys—that there is more than one—you, as a born again Son
of God, have been given the authority and the right to unlock and enter into
the Kingdom of Heaven, where is found all of the mystery of God. The word
"heaven" as used here is the same Greek word to denote where God dwells.

Keys are a symbol of power and authority. God has given us these keys
and it should be no mystery to us how to enter into and operate in the
spiritual realm. Throughout the Bible we have been given directions on how
God expects us to live our life and carry out our mission in life. God had each
one of us on His mind before He ever created the earth. He has equipped us
with everything that we would ever need in this life but He has hidden it in
His Word for us to dig out and apply.

The most important key for us to find is just what is already bound and
loosed in heaven, and to apply those principals in our lives here on this earth.
It is your responsibility to do the binding and loosening. As you work your

way through this study guide, you will recognize those things in your life that are displeasing to God.

To "bind," from the Greek word *deo*, means to bind, be in bonds, knit, fasten, tie, and wind. This word is related to *deomia*, meaning to petition, beseech, make request, and pray. To bind also means to obligate yourself to someone—which we will discuss later.

To "loose," from the Greek word *luo*, means to loosen, break up, destroy, dissolve, unloosen, melt, and put off. *Luo* is closely related to *rhegnumi* and *agnumi*, which mean to break, wreck, crack to sunder by separation of its parts, shatter to minute fragments, disrupt, lacerate, convulse, burst, rend, and tear.

This binding and loosing forms the very basic principal of walking the Christian walk. Life is all about decisions and when you decided to make Jesus your Lord and Savior you unlocked and opened the door of salvation into the Kingdom of heaven. Now you face the decision to move forward into the kingdom or just stay where you are. I want to encourage you to step out and take all that God has provided for you.

What you are seeing here forms only the very basic principal of the keys of binding and loosing. As your walk with Christ matures you will need to get a broader understanding of the subject which is accomplished by receiving a broader meaning of the words.

You are probably telling yourself you will never be able to do this—which is fear! With a little Bible study, we find out it is God's will for us to "fear not," and in II Timothy 1:7, we see "God has not given us the spirit of fear; but of power, and of love, and of a sound mind." We know faith is the direct opposite of fear and "Faith is the substance of things hoped for, the evidence of things not seen" (Hebrews 11:1). We know "Faith comes by hearing the word of God" (Romans 10:17). So to overcome our fear (which is an attitude) of not being able to carry out the assignment God has given us, we must concentrate on the Word of God that tells us: ". . . all things are possible to him that believeth"; "I can do all things through Christ which strengthens me" (Mark 9:23); and "I have strength for all things in Christ Who empowers me [I am ready for anything and equal to anything through Him Who infuses inner strength into me; I am self-sufficient in Christ's sufficiency]" (Philippians 4:13 AMP); "I am strong in the Lord and the power of His might" (Ephesians 6:10). And, most of all, because I have Christ in me, "I can do exceeding abundantly above all that I ask or think, according to the power of God that works in me" (Ephesians 3:20). That power is your faith!

That power, from the Greek word *exousia,* means physical and mental power; the ability or strength with which one is endued, which he either possesses or exercises [Luke 24:49].

This book is a prime example of what you have just read. When God instructed me to write this book, I just flat-out told Him, out of ignorance and fear, that I couldn't and wouldn't do it because I was not qualified. Over a period of time, however, I learned to put the Word of God to work for me by driving out that spirit of fear and not allowing it to work in my life. Then I tied myself to God and all the blessings Jesus has provided for me by yielding myself to the Holy Spirit and allowing Him to lead and guide me into all truth—all I had to do was listen to what He was telling me, write it out, and give Him all of the credit (I Corinthians 2:10).

I discovered, in Matthew 12:36—37, that I would be judged by every idle (inoperative, nonworking) word that I spoke. For by my words I will be justified and acquitted, and by my words I would be condemned and sentenced. So it was up to me to determine just what words would come out of my mouth. By taking God's Word and forming confessions of faith and by continually making those confessions, I was able to turn God's power loose in my life and break the hold (fear) the devil had on me.

In the end you are to bind the spirit of fear from your life by resisting the devil, which is done by quoting the Word of God to the devil. Fear is bound in heaven because it is not from God and then you must loose on earth that which is from God, the spirit of power, love, and a sound mind. And then you must embrace or surround yourself with faith and the love of God because, "There is no fear in love; but perfect love casteth out fear" (I John 4:18). Simply put, you need only to pray and surround yourself with the love of God and let that love take care of any fear that might be in your life! The key is to close the door to demonic activity. I Peter 5:8 tells us the devil walks about seeking whom he may devour, and he is able to do this by simply listening to the words which proceed from your mouth.

But James 4:7 (NIV) tells us you just need to "Submit yourself, then, to God, resist the devil and he will flee from you." You must submit yourself (be subject to) God, then you must resist (stand firm against) the devil. Then and only then, will he will flee from you as if in terror. It probably won't happen overnight, so you must be determined to stay in for the long run.

Almost everyone comes to Christ with baggage, which Jesus called traditions (Matthew 15:2), and Paul referred to as strongholds (II Corinthians 10:4) that need to be pulled down or eliminated from our lives or they will invalidate the Word of God (Mark 7:13 NAS). Traditions or strongholds are preconceived ideas and misconceptions about God or anything we rely upon to defend our opinions or positions even though they either have no basis in the Bible or an incorrect one. Many of these strongholds stem from wrong patterns of thinking, attitudes and behaviors, ideas, desires, and habits.

The weapons we have been given, binding and loosing, are mighty, through God, in the pulling down of these strongholds (II Corinthians 10:4). But to use them, you must get yourself into a position where you hear from, listen to God, and obey His instructions (John 2:5). This is what it means to be "strong in the lord and the power of His might." You turn away from the world's ways of doing things and operate in the authority God has given to you. Romans 12:2 (AMP) puts it this way; "Do not be conformed to this world (this age), [fashioned after and adapted to its external, superficial customs], but be transformed (changed) by the [entire] renewal of your mind [by its new ideals and its new attitudes], so that you may prove [for yourselves] what is the good and acceptable and perfect will of God, even the thing which is good and acceptable and perfect [in His sight for you]."

In Matthew 6:10, we see it is God's desire that, "His will be done in earth, as it is in heaven." So, it is up to you to find out just what is the good and perfect will of God, (it's in the Word of God), apply it to your life by walking in His will to the best of your ability, and allowing the Holy Spirit to direct your words and actions. Two excellent places to start looking are found in Romans 12:9-21 and I Thessalonians 5:16-22.

UNDERSTANDING FEAR:

Be careful to not confuse the spirit of fear and the emotion called fear and the fear of God. There is a difference between the spirit of fear and the emotion called fear. If you confuse them, you can put yourself into a state of confusion and worry. God's Word tells us many times to "fear not" because if you don't learn to conquer fear, it will conquer you (Isaiah 41:10).

There is an emotion of fear that is God-given to help you, and there is the spirit of fear—made up of what are commonly called phobias—which come from the devil. They are two entirely different kinds of fear that are for two entirely different purposes.

We all need to know how to bridle the emotion of fear, learn how to allow it to help us master our moods, and help us accomplish our mission. Healthy fear is an asset to life and all we are to accomplish.

The spirit of fear comes from Satan, the prince of darkness. When you choose to live in darkness, Satan is your prince—prince, meaning someone who has authority. When you choose to live in darkness, Satan has the authority to run your life. And when you reject darkness and choose to live in the light, as Christ is in the light, you have the joy of following the light of the world.

It's your choice whether you live in the kingdom of light or the kingdom of darkness. You either choose Jesus or Satan to be your master.

The spirit of fear comes into your life by sin and is sustained by sin and like a virus it will invade your soul and require more evil in which it might live. Sin gives fear a license to rule your life. Fear attacks your mind telling you that you are too tired to try again, you are too weak to win, and you are too exhausted to endure.

To overcome the spirit of fear, you need to take charge of your life and confess that you are a child of God, an ambassador of the Lord Jesus Christ, and you need to think like an ambassador and live like one. If you will stand on the Word of God, your faith will tell you: "We are more than conquerors through Christ, Nothing is impossible with God. For they that wait upon the Lord shall renew their strength, they shall mount up on wings as eagles; they shall run, and not grow weary; and they shall walk, and not faint; For God is with me" (Romans 8:37; Luke 1:37; Isaiah 40:31).

There are many benefits to be had from practicing the fear of the Lord. He who fears God has a built-in restraint against yielding to anything evil. In other words, one "thinks twice" before doing or saying anything they know to be wrong. The fear of God works well with Holy Spirit conviction. Reverential respect of God and Holy Spirit conviction helps one stay out of trouble and be aware of God's divine order for their life.

> The Fear of the Lord prolongs days, but the years of the wicked shall be shortened (Proverbs 10:27, 8:13, 9:10).

> The Fear of the Lord is a fountain of life, to depart from the snares of death (Proverbs 14:27).

> Better is little with the fear of the Lord than great treasure and trouble there with (Proverbs 15:16, 14:26-27, 15:33, 19:23).

The fear of God is a characteristic that should be natural to mankind, both saint and sinner. It's your choice.

An example: In the Garden of Eden, Eve allowed Satan's cunning lie to override her fear of God. Adam's natural love for Eve overrode his fear of God. Look at the trouble their lack of fear has brought upon mankind. Noah and his family evidently feared God and obeyed Him. Noah, without fear could have reasoned himself out of the assignment to build an ark; after all, it had never rained. Noah feared God and was obedient, thus saving mankind from total destruction.

Maintaining a healthy respect and reverence for God produces wonderful results! Numerous things may reflect a loss of the Fear of God. One's thoughts and actions of carnality, materialism, worldly pleasures, and lust indicate the fear of God is diminished. Consider the immorality now in our country and in our churches and you can quickly realize that there is no fear of God which is only found in a personal relationship with Jesus Christ.

MEDITATING ON THE WORD OF GOD:

Another key to understanding the Kingdom of Heaven is found in Joshua 1:8.

> This book of the law shall not depart of thy mouth, but thou shalt meditate therein day and night, that thou mayest observe to do according to all that is written therein; for then shall thou make thy way prosperous, and then thou shalt have good success.

Note: "Thy" and "thou" in this verse means, of course, "your" and "you". It is up to you to determine how much you will prosper and have good success in your life and walk with God. God's limits are for you to be blessed "exceeding abundantly above all that you can ask or think" (Ephesians 3:20). And your goal should be to experience the "exceeding greatness of His power toward us who believe according to the working of His mighty power. Which he wrought in Christ, when he raised him from the dead, and set him at his own right hand in the heavenly places" (Ephesians 1:19-20).

Jesus has instructed us in Matthew 22:37, "Thou shalt love the Lord thy God with all thy heart, and with all thy soul, and with all thy mind." And in Romans 8:6-7 we are told "To be carnally minded is death; but to be spiritually minded is life and peace. Because the carnal mind is enmity against God: for it is not subject to the law of God, either indeed can be."

In I Peter 1:13 and I Corinthians 2:16 (NIV) we are told to, ". . . prepare our mind for action," because, ". . . we have the mind of Christ."

You must bind your will, your thoughts, and your life to the will of God. Bind your days, your nights, and the work of your hands to the will of God. Bind yourself to the truth of God's Word. Bind yourself to a conscious awareness of the blood of Jesus and its "healing power, its protection, its covering, and cleansing."

In Ephesians 4:16 another word meaning "to bind" also means to compact. (*sumbiazo* from the Greek) "From whom (Christ) the whole body fitly joined together and compacted (bound together) by that which every joint supplieth, according to the effectual working in the measure of every part, maketh increase of the body unto the edifying of itself in love." The word "compacted" here means to cause to coalesce, to join together, and to put together into one whole. Binding your mind to Christ's mind is a powerful key in situations which you really don't know what is going on. You must bind your mind to the mind of Christ and take your thoughts captive to the Word of God. Believe that Christ's mind, by the Holy Spirit, is feeding supernatural input into your mind. Philippians 2:5 directs us to "Let this mind be in you, which was also in Christ Jesus." And I Corinthians 2:16 tells us, "But we have the mind of Christ." What are you doing with it?

Binding your mind to the mind of Christ will also help you line up with II Corinthians 10:5: "Casting down imaginations, and every high thing that exalteth itself against the knowledge of God, and bringing into captivity every thought to the obedience of Christ." You must learn to let Christ's mind, by the Holy Spirit, feed supernatural input into your mind.

Binding your mind to the mind of Christ is a powerful key in situations which you do not know what is going on, as I said earlier, or how to meet either the revealed or the hidden expectations of others.

In Ephesians 6:10 we are directed to "Finally [This is final, we must do this now] be strong in the Lord, and in the power of <u>His</u> might." By using the key of binding through prayer, you activate the process of being strengthened by Christ in every area of your life. You will soon recognize you are getting understanding in situations that are simply not discernible in the natural (John 14:2).

Here we can clearly see we are to love God with our entire mind because being spiritually minded is life and peace; but to be carnally minded is death and is enmity or hostile against God and will not allow us to please Him. God has given us the mind of Christ so we may know His thoughts and His ways and we are to prepare it for action by putting our mind in agreement with the mind of Christ (John 14:12; Isaiah 55:8-9).

Now we know to be carnally minded, which is enmity against God, is already bound in heaven. It is up to us to bind it here on the earth by meditating the Word of God day and night. We must become spiritually minded for life and peace, which means preparing our mind action. By thus transforming our mind from being carnal to being spiritually minded we are loosening it, declaring it lawful here on the earth because we know that it is already loosed in heaven.

II Peter 1:3-4 (AMP) tells us:

> For His divine power has bestowed upon us all things that [are requisite and suited] to life and godliness, through the [full personal] knowledge of Him who called us by and to His own glory and excellence (virtue).
>
> By means of these He has bestowed on us His precious and exceedingly great promises, so that through them you may escape [by flight] from the moral decay (rottenness and corruption) that is in the world because of covetousness (lust and greed) and become sharers (partakers) of the divine nature.

If you want God's best for your life, you must be willing to be a partaker of and a participant in God's divine nature. This will require you to bind yourself to the truth and to God's will for your life, bind yourself to a conscious awareness of the blood of Jesus and the works of the cross, turn your back on the world's way of doing things and make the change to God's way, so you might experience God's divine power that He wants to bestow on you. This will allow you to experience a personal knowledge of He who has called you to His own glory and excellence. It's your choice!

Psalm 1:2-3 tells us that to the man who is seeking God, ". . . his delight is in the law of the Lord: and in his law doth he meditate day and night."

If you will take the time to crave God's Word and feed on it, your faith will grow and God will be able to use you more and more. A strong desire for God's Word is a dominant characteristic of the person who is blessed. Psalm 105:3-4 in the Amplified Bible says:

Glory in His holy name; let the hearts of those rejoice who seek and require the Lord [as their indispensable necessity].

Seek, inquire of and for the Lord, and crave Him and His strength (His might and inflexibility to temptation); seek and require His face and His presence [continually] evermore.

Once you taste and see that the Lord is good, you will forever crave Him and seek out ways to continually feed on His Word. And when you do, you will be like the man in Psalm 1:3. "And he shall be like a tree planted by the rivers of water, that bringeth forth his fruit in his season; his leaf also shall not wither; and whatever he doeth shall prosper." [Jeremiah 17:7-10.] The results will be you living a fruitful, long, and prosperous life! If you are planted firmly in God's Word and tended to by His refreshing living water, you are primed and ready to bring forth fruit! Instead of fading out or withering away, you have God's promise that everything you do will prosper.

In Proverbs 4:20-23 (AMP) God instructs us to:

My son attend [take or give heed] to my words; incline thine ear unto my sayings [be ready to change, be ready to believe].

Let them not depart from thine eyes; Keep them in the midst of thine heart.

For they are life unto those that find them, and health to all their flesh.

Keep and guard your heart with all vigilance and above all that you guard, for out of it flows the springs of life.

God's will is for you to be like those described in Psalm 92:12-14.

The righteous shall flourish like the palm tree: he shall grow like a cedar in Lebanon.

Those that be planted in the house of the Lord shall flourish in the courts of our God.

They shall still bring forth fruit in old age; they shall be fat and flourishing.

Meditation on God's Word will reveal to you who God is, and who you are "in Christ," and all of the blessings He has in store for you (II Corinthians 5:17; Galatians 3:13).

Being in Christ is knowing and understanding that the fullness of God is living on the inside of you (Colossians 2:9).

It's your choice! God is no respecter of persons, and what God said to Joshua will work for everyone. Ask yourself, if God didn't want Joshua to be prosperous, why did He tell him how to prosper? If God didn't want Joshua to be successful, why did He tell him how to have good success? But God wanted Joshua to be prosperous and successful and He also wants you to be prosperous and successful (Psalm 35:27)! But to do so you will have to spend quality time meditating in the Word of God.

It is vitally important for all Christians to spend time meditating in the word of God, not so much seeking revelation knowledge but seeking to know God and Jesus and learning how to please Him. Matthew 7:24 (NKJV) says, "Therefore whoever hears these sayings of Mine, and <u>does them</u>, I will liken him to a wise man who built his house upon the rock."

If you ever want to fulfill what God has called you to do, you must first take the time to meditate in the word of God. Start with just a few minutes several times a day and work up from there. The best times for me at first included a few minutes after I woke in the morning, the last few minutes before I went to sleep at night, and while I was driving to and from work.

God promised that if you would spend quality time in His Word He would make your way prosperous, and then you shalt have good success (Joshua 1:8). Remember, "The Lord is not slack concerning his promise, as some men count slackness; but is longsuffering to us-ward, not willing that any should perish, but that all should come to repentance" (II Peter 3:9).

What do you think about, or what do you mediate on; positive thoughts, empowering thoughts, affirming thoughts, or negative defeating thoughts? It's your choice! Philippians 4:8-9 tells us what God recommends for us to be thinking about.

> Finally, brethren, whatsoever things are true, whatsoever things are honest, whatsoever things are just, whatsoever things are pure, whatsoever things are lovely, whatsoever thing are of good report; if there be any virtue, and if there be any praise, think on these things.

Those things, which ye have both learned, and received and heard, and seen in me do: and the God of peace shall be with you.

If you will spend time meditating on the Word of God and allow it to tenderize your heart to the place where you begin to practice the presence of God and begin to hear His voice, the Holy Spirit will then begin to lead and guide you into all truth and start showing you things to come (John 16:13; I Corinthians 2:10).

WHO DO YOU ASSOCIATE WITH?

Another key to developing your faith is to watch the company you keep. You have to make sure you don't surround yourself with people who think and speak negatively. Proverbs 14:6-15 The Message Bible, tells us:

> Cynics look high and low for wisdom—and never find it; the open-minded find it right on their doorstep!
>
> Escape quickly from the company of fools; they're a waste of your time, a waste of your words.
>
> The wisdom of the wise keeps life on track; the foolishness of fools lands them in the ditch.
>
> The stupid ridicule right and wrong, but a moral life is a favored life.
>
> The person who shuns the bitter moments of friends will be an outsider at their celebrations.
>
> Lives of careless wrongdoing are tumbledown shacks; holy living builds soaring cathedrals.
>
> There's a way of life that looks harmless enough; look again—it leads straight to hell. Sure those people appear to be having a good time, but all that laughter will end in heartbreak.

The best thing you can do is keep company with people who are more tuned in with and turned on to God than you are. These are the kind of people who will help you develop your faith. Choose friends who believe God and know how to stand fast—even in the most difficult of times. If you want to develop great faith, seek out people who are full of faith and are led by the Holy Spirit and stick with them! You will have to help each other. Once you have developed your own faith, you will be in a position to start helping others who are growing in faith. But always be connected to someone who has stronger faith than you because: "The man who through faith is just and upright shall live and shall live by faith" (Romans 1:17 AMP; Colossians 2:8; Mark 16:17-18).

Psalm 1:1 tells us that, "Blessed is the man that walked not in the counsel of the ungodly, nor standeth in the way of sinners, nor sitteth in the seat of the scornful."

To be blessed means to be "empowered to prosper". This verse is a warning flag to all Christians. It is difficult to thrive when ungodly sinners who have no respect for and mock God, continually surround you. It may be possible for you to survive in that environment, but you may never reach your greatest potential as a Son of God hanging with the wrong crowd. It will stunt your spiritual growth and rob you of the power to prosper. You must choose not to hang out with the wrong crowd, because the people that you associate with do influence you greatly!

This verse is also a warning for us to be careful of where we go to church and school and who we allow to teach or instruct us.

2

THE KEY OF LOVE

Probably the most important Key to the kingdom of God is the Key of Love. For walking in love, the God kind of love, is the key to the fullness of God's blessings in your life.

"For God so loved the world that he gave his only begotten son, that whosoever believeth in him shall not perish but have everlasting life" (John 3:16). Probably the most famous scripture in the Bible is all about God's amazing love for us. And in Romans 5:8-11 (AMP) we are told:

> . . . God shows and clearly proves His [own] love for us by the fact that while we were still sinners, Christ (the Messiah, the Anointed One) died for us.
>
> Therefore, since we are now justified (acquitted, made righteous, and brought into right relationship with God) by Christ's blood, how much more [certain is it that] we shall be saved by Him from the indignation and wrath of God.
>
> For if while we were enemies we were reconciled to God through the death of His son, it is much more [certain], now that we are reconciled, that we shall be saved (daily delivered from sin's dominion) through His [resurrection] life.
>
> Not only so, but we also rejoice and exultingly glory in God [in His love and perfection] through our Lord Jesus Christ through Whom we have now received and enjoy [our] reconciliation.

And that is not all! In Colossians 1:12-14 (AMP) we are told that God:

Who has qualified and made us fit to share the portion which is the inheritance of the saints (God's holy people in the Light).

[The Father] has delivered and drawn us to Himself out of the control and the dominion of darkness and has transferred us into the kingdom of the Son of His love.

In whom we have our redemption through His blood, [which means] the forgiveness of our sins.

These are just three of the benefits of being a Christian! But along with these benefits come responsibilities. In I John 3:23 we see where it is God's will for our lives that we "Should believe on the name of his Son Jesus Christ, and love one another, as he gave us commandment."

II Peter 1:3-9 (AMP) tells us God has given us everything we will ever need for life and godliness.

For His divine power has bestowed upon us all things that [are requisite and suited] to life and godliness, through the [full, personal] knowledge of Him Who called us by and to His own glory and excellence (virtue).

By means of these He has bestowed on us His precious and exceedingly great promises, so that through them you may escape [by flight] from the moral decay (rottenness and corruption) that is in the world because of covetousness (lust and greed), and become sharers (partakers) of the divine nature.

For this very reason, adding your diligence [to the divine promises], employ every effort in exercising your faith to develop virtue (excellence, resolution, Christian energy), and in [exercising] virtue [develop] knowledge (intelligence),

And in [exercising] knowledge [develop] self-control, and in [exercising] self-control [develop] steadfastness (patience, endurance) and in [exercising] steadfastness [develop godliness (piety)],

And in [exercising] godliness [develop] brotherly affection, and in [exercising] brotherly affection [develop] Christian love.

> For as these qualities are yours and increasingly abound
> in you, they will keep [you] from being idle or unfruitful
> unto the [full personal] knowledge of our Lord Jesus Christ
> (the Messiah, the Anointed One).
> For whoever lacks these qualities is blind, [spiritually]
> shortsighted, seeing only what is near to him, and has
> become oblivious [to the fact] that he was cleansed from his
> old sins.

Stop and think about what you have just read. God's goodness is the foundation of everything He wants you to accomplish in this life, and it is yours for the taking. Psalm 106:1 tells us "God is good," and Psalm 145:8-9 tells us "The Lord is gracious, and full of compassion; slow to anger, and of great mercy. The Lord is good to all: and his tender mercies are over all his works." This means God wants us, you and me, to experience things that are truly good. And in Psalm 34:8 we are invited to, "Taste and see that the Lord is good. Blessed is the man who takes refuge in Him." God is inviting you to come and live in His presence and experience His goodness. God is not mad at you; nor will He send you away from Him in anger. God is love, and He loves you just as much as He loves Jesus. His desire is for you to have a father-son relationship with Him. He wants you to experience an intimate relationship with Him. He wants you to bring all of your problems and hurts to Him so He can shower His great love and mercy upon you. He has extended to you a personal invitation to be with Him to experience all of His goodness. The question is, what are you going to do about it? It is your choice! Life is full of choices, and Deuteronomy 30:19 makes it clear God has put the choice up to you.

James 1:16-17 tells us we should always keep ourselves on guard least we be tricked into forgetting that "every good and perfect gift" is from God. Always remember, anytime you ever experience something good in your life; it was a gift from God. It is so easy to forget God's desire is that you experience things which are truly good. He continually invites us to be lifted to a new and higher level of life through His goodness. Again, the choice is yours as to how much of the goodness of God you want to experience! Understand, there is plenty for everybody. The key to getting more in your life is by taking what God has given you and sharing it with others because the more you give it away, the more you will experience it yourself!

Everywhere you go these days, people are hurting and discouraged; many have broken dreams. They've made mistakes and their lives are in a mess. They need to feel God's compassion and goodness and experience His unconditional love. They don't need you to judge and criticize them. They need you to bring hope, to bring healing, and to show God's mercy. Really, they are looking for a good friend, somebody who will be there to encourage them, to take the time to listen to their story, and genuinely care for them in their time of need.

This world is crying out for people with compassion who will love unconditionally, people who will take some of their precious time to help their fellow man. When God created you, He put His supernatural love into your heart. He placed in you the potential to have a kind, caring, gentle, and loving spirit. Because you were created in God's image, you have the moral capacity to experience God's compassion in your heart, and if you want to live your best life now, you must make sure that you keep your heart of compassion open. You will need to be on the outlook for people who you can bless. You need to be willing to be interrupted and be inconvenienced if it means you can help meet the need of somebody else. As God's representative on this earth, you have this opportunity to make a difference in the lives of other people but you must first learn to follow God's instructions and the leading of the Holy Spirit in your life.

Saving that which was lost or saving those who do not know Him is the primary objective of our Lord and Savior, Jesus Christ. Many people know about God, but they do not know God! You can tell if someone knows God by his actions. God is love and those who know Him obey His Word.

My ultimate goal is to persuade you "that neither death nor life, nor angels, nor principalities, nor powers, nor things present, nor things to come, nor height, nor depth, nor any other creature, shall be able to separate you from the love of God which is in Christ Jesus our Lord" (Romans 8:38-39).

God's will is for each one of us to "walk in love, as Christ also hath loved us, and hath given himself for us an offering and a sacrifice to God for a sweet-smelling savor" (Ephesians 5:2).

People want love to be easy and or to be fair. Sometimes love requires you to give one hundred percent of yourself while the other person gives nothing. Jesus did it. He went to the cross. He was rejected by His own people, abandoned by His friends, and knew that many more generations would also reject Him. Yet He gave one hundred percent while we gave nothing. What kind of love moved God to send His son to pay the price for our sins? What kind of love endured the brutality and rejection of the cross? That same love of God that loved Jesus, loves you. If God didn't spare His own son, how will He not freely give you all things? You can trust God because God is faithful (Romans 8:32; I Corinthians 1:9; Hebrews 2:17).

God has a plan for your life. When you discover just what it is, it will set you free to pursue your mission in life. God desires you to have a loving relationship with Him, and it is never too late to get into the will of God! He does not desire for you to go to hell. He created you for His glory and for everlasting fellowship. You are His creation, and He loves you. God desires for you to not "forget the assembling of yourselves." He desires that you come together and pray and study His Word and worship Him in the spirit of holiness (Isaiah 43:7; Hebrews 10:25; Colossians 1:9-14, 2:7; I Timothy 2:4; II Peter 3:9).

God's Word is so simple to understand that one has to work at not being able to understand it. So don't deny the Holy Ghost the right to place on your life the desire for what God has for you. Let God do for and through you what He desires to do. Yield yourself to God today, and get a vision of what God has planned for you, because you are the one in control of what goes into your eyes and ears. You are responsible for what gets into your heart and ultimately for what you believe. Put your eyes and ears on the Word of God. Receive it and believe it. This is how faith comes (Romans 10:17). Faith is simply believing and acting on God's Word. Faith is not mental assent or mental agreement. It is when you act on God's Word that it becomes a reality. No matter what the problem is, God's Word has something to say about it. God's Word has the answer. It is your responsibility to find out what the Word says, and act on it (James 2:17).

God is not going to tell you to live by faith and then fail to tell you how to do it. You simply have to continue to keep His Word in front of your eyes and in your ears. What you hear and see gets down into your heart. Whether good things or bad things, what you focus on becomes what you believe. So focus on what the Word of God says and you will have victory in every situation (John 1:12; Romans 10:17).

God's desire is not to punish but to heal, not to condemn but to restore, not to banish but to reconcile, not to torment but to encourage. God is an infinitely forgiving and merciful Father! God the Father is the wooing, loving and forgiving (Abba) father of Jesus Christ, and He desires to be your spiritual Father also (Galatians 4:6.).

Pray: "Father, reveal to me the fullness of who you truly are and help me to learn to call You Father just as Jesus does, and to know you as He knows you. In Jesus' Name."

Jesus did not come to save humankind from God, but to lead everyone to God. He wants to help you acknowledge Almighty God as your Father, and accept your place as His son. Experiencing the love the Father has for His children is what life is all about, although I don't believe that very many Christians ever discover it.

Do you want your Christian life to be effective and bear fruit? Then follow the instructions in II Peter 1:5-7: Be diligent concerning God's promises, exercise your faith to develop virtue, grow in knowledge, increase in self-control, be steadfast, practice goodliness, and show Christian love to others.

Hebrews 3:1 tells us Jesus Christ is the "Apostle and High Priest of our profession." The word "Profession" can also be translated "confession" and it refers to the words that we speak. Its literal translation is "to say the same thing." Jesus now sits at the right hand of Almighty God (Ephesians 1:20) and it is one of His duties to cause or bring to pass the words we speak when we make confessions of faith based on the Word of God. Jesus has delivered us from the curse of the law (Galatians 3:13), but He can not cause our words of doubt and unbelief to come to pass. "For whatever is not of faith is sin" (Romans 14:23). And: "We know that God does not listen to sinners; but if anyone is God-fearing and a worshiper of Him and does His will, He listens to him" (John 9:31 AMP).

Through His death and Resurrection He has already provided us with absolute victory in every area of our life. So from this moment on, never make a confession of faith that is not based on the Word of God.

Confess: "In Him was life; and that life was the light of men. That life in is in me, that life is developing my spirit. I have the wisdom of God and revelation knowledge flows into me continually. For Jesus is my wisdom and I walk in the light of life!" (John 1:4, 8:12; I Corinthians 1:30; Ephesians 1:17).

Note: My object in giving you confessions of faith is to show you how to operate in the principles of God's Word. Proverbs 18:21 tells us that, "Death and life are in the power of the tongue: and they that love it shall eat the fruit thereof."

God's Word conceived in your heart, then formed with your tongue and spoken out of your mouth will become a spiritual force releasing the ability of God in and for you. These are words that you first conceive in your spirit and then you form them with your tongue. The Word of God conceived in your human spirit, then formed with your tongue and spoken out of your mouth, releases the ability of God. This is how God intended for you to receive His Word. You can also receive and speak other words. For instance, if it's the devil you are quoting, you are releasing the ability of the devil. Your words that are not in agreement with the Word of God are what give the devil his power to work in your life.

The Word of God that you conceive on the inside of you and speak out of your mouth will set the cornerstone of your life. God's words are the most powerful things in the universe and you have the ability to give voice to them. John 1:1-3 (AMP) says,

> In the beginning [before all time] was the Word (Christ), and the Word was with God, and the Word was God Himself.
>
> He was present originally with God.
>
> All things were made and came into existence through Him; and without Him was not even one thing made that has come into being.

You have the authority to speak God's words after Him. There is no authority exercised without words. And God has given you authority over the devil and all of his powers (Luke 10:19).

Take time now to ask God to, "set a watch over your mouth and keep the door of your lips" (Psalm 141:3).

You must realize God knows what He is talking about and if you will do what He says, you will have what He said you can have. So, don't be just a hearer of the Word, but also be a doer of God's Word, for the Word of God is the power of God unto salvation [deliverance from eternal death, preservation, healing and soundness] (Romans 1:16).

Being a hearer and a doer of God's Word will cause you to not only please God but allow you to reap great rewards in the here and now.

Psalms 37:4-5 instructs us to "Delight thyself also in the Lord; and he shall give thee the desires of thine heart, Commit thy way unto the Lord; trust also in him; and he shall bring it to pass."

When you come to a place where you serve God for pure love's sake, you will find the hand of the Lord upon you, and you will never fail in your endeavor.

3

THE GOD KIND OF LOVE

God is love (I John 4:8).
God is light (John 8:12; I John 1:5).
God is life (Amos 5:4).
God is a Spirit (John 4:24).
God is a good God (Psalm 106:1; 145:9).
God's Word is eternal (Hebrews 13:8).
God's Word is Truth (John 17:17).
God's Word is pure (James 3:17).
God's Word is Life (John 1:4-5).

God's Word is the key to life, it is not a way of life, it is the way of life, it is the only life there is!

God and His Word are all of these things to those who will receive them. God has never changed. His Word has never changed or lost its power to produce what He said. However, as always, it takes the power of faith filled with Love to activate it and keep it working until one becomes whole, wanting nothing.

God is a spirit being, and you and I have been made in the image of God and after His likeness. We are spirit beings which live in a body, and we possess a soul, which consists of our mind, will, and emotions. With our spirits we contact the spiritual world. With our body we contact the physical world. And with our soul we contact the intellectual world. These are the only three realms we can contact (John 4:24, Genesis 1:26-27; I Corinthians 15:50; II Corinthians 4:16; I Thessalonians 5:23; I Peter 3:4).

God created us to be different from one another, and He did it on purpose. Each of us meets a different need, and we are all part of God's overall plan. God wants us to fit into His plan, not to feel pressured to try and fit into everyone else's plans. Different is okay because it is all right to be different. Be who God created you to be!

You belong to God and knowing that truth will give you confidence, which will enable you to do more for God and allow you to see yourself complete "in Christ" (Ephesians 2:10).

When you were born again, God became your Father. God is a love God. You are born of God and God is love; therefore, you are born of love. The nature of God is in you and the nature of God is love.

When you confessed Jesus Christ as your lord and savior—when you were born-again, you became a new creature in Christ Jesus, and you moved into a place of right-standing with the God of the universe. Your right-standing or righteousness with God gives you the right and ability to stand in His presence without a sense of sin, guilt, fear, inferiority, or condemnation. You now have just as much right to stand before God as Jesus does. You have been made the righteousness of God in Christ Jesus and this righteousness brings peace, fellowship, faith and it restores son ship, which will allow you to walk and talk with God in fellowship—just like Adam experienced before the fall.

You are to awaken to righteousness and sin not because your righteousness does not come by the way you act. Righteousness is the nature of God, and when you join in with the nature of God, your actions will become right, because that right way of acting is your conduct, which is holiness.

How does God see you? He sees you through the blood of Jesus. He sees you as a covenant son, complete, having all of your needs met because there is no condemnation to those who are in Christ Jesus. He calls you the head and not the tail and when you awake to this, it will awaken a new boldness on the inside of you. You will see yourself as God sees you, which will allow you to walk and talk to God on a father-son basis. God's ears are open to the righteous, and "The earnest (heartfelt, continued) prayer of a righteousness man makes tremendous power available [dynamic in its working]" (James 5:16 AMP). A person who is doing good things, God's will, will have his prayers answered. "The works of the righteous shall be peace; and the effect of righteousness quietness and assurance forever" (Isaiah 32:17). That is just one of the rights He purchased for you because God wants to finish the course with you. He wants you to be complete and content, and He will continue until you get to where He is taking you. He doesn't want you to be a little happy, slightly blessed, or partly healed. He wants your life to be dominated by joy and He wants your joy to be full. He wants you to live in abundance, and He wants to give you the desire of your heart

(Colossians 1:12-13; Ephesians 1:3-4; II Corinthians 5:17; Hebrews 4:16; Romans 5:19-21).

Another right He purchased for you is to walk the same love walk that Jesus walked. God hand-picked you before the foundation of the world, and if God is for you—and He is, according to Roman 8:31—who can effectively be against you? (Romans 8:29-31; Colossians 2:10). Nobody can stand against God or you when your faith and confidence are in Christ! Faith simply believes what God says about any circumstances in your life, rather than believing what you feel, what you see, or what you hear. The truth is, if you will get in agreement with God, this can be the greatest time of your life.

With God on your side, you cannot possibly lose. He can make a way when it looks as though there is no way. He can open doors no man can shut. He can cause you to be at the right place, at the right time and He can supernaturally turn your life around.

God expects you to open up your heart and walk with Him in faith. When you do, He will reward you beyond your wildest expectations. He is working actively on your behalf. He is standing up for you. He is supplying all of your needs. Out of the treasury of His abundant grace, He is giving you His wisdom and His ability.

I Corinthians 3:9 calls us "labourers together with God . . ." That's fellowship with the Father! He supplies us with strength, wisdom, grace, and ability—the supernatural tools with which we work as able ministers of the New Covenant.

Hebrews 11:6 tells us "Without faith it is impossible to please him; for he that cometh to God must believe that he is, and that he is a rewarder of them that diligently seek him." The greatest stumbling block to one's faith is a lack of a good understanding of God's Word, and all hindrances to one's faith are centered around this lack of knowledge (Hosea 4:6). You cannot believe or have faith beyond your actual knowledge of the Word of God. Faith in God's Word always produces results! The Word of God that you continue to place in your heart through your eyes and your ears—the Word that you speak in agreement with God—will increase your faith, and your faith will automatically grow as your understanding of God's Word grows (Romans 10:17). If your faith is not growing, it's because your knowledge of God's Word is not growing, and you cannot grow or develop spiritually if you are not willing to spend quality time in the Word of God and grow in faith (Psalm 119:130).

Faith keeps us moving in the direction and on the path God has planned for our lives. We hear, we believe, we speak, we receive, and we get there! Faith in God's Word will always produce results!

Your goal should be to get so full of the Word that it becomes bigger in you than the situation that you are facing. So start dwelling on these things and allow them to become a reality in you. When it becomes a reality in your spirit, you will quote I John 4:4: "Greater is he that is in me than he that is in the world," with an assurance you have never known before. You will realize you are not the victim any more but the victor, you are blessed and cannot be cursed, and you are more than a conqueror (Romans 8:37). As more than a conqueror you are a winner and there is nothing in life which can defeat you. You can take back those areas and things of your life the devil has stolen from you and live in the fullness of life. We all know Satan is against us, but the question we must ask ourselves is; are we going to agree with God or with the devil? You know the answer, so stop opposing yourself and mentally beating yourself up just because Satan is against you!

Psalm 34:19 (AMP) tells us "Many evils comfort the [consistently] righteous, but the Lord delivers him out of them all." Remember, the devil has been completely defeated at Calvary; he has been rejected and is awaiting his confinement in the lake of fire for eternity (Revelation 20:10; I Peter 5:8).

Enforce the devil's defeat and incorporate what belongs to you. Confess: "Jesus died for me! Jesus arose victorious over death, hell and the grave—and He did that for me! The Lord is my light and my salvation; whom shall if fear? The Lord is the strength of my life; of whom shall I be afraid? Therefore, I am strong in the Lord and the power of His might. The Word of God lives in me and I have overcome the wicked one. Jesus conquered and arose victorious over Satan for me! Therefore, Satan has no dominion over me! I'm free, because I am complete in Him, in Christ, which is the head of all principality and power!" (Ephesians 6:10; Philippians 1:6; Colossians 2:10).

Now it is time for you to ". . . be strong in the Lord [be empowered through your union with Him]; draw your strength from Him [that strength which His boundless might provides]" (Ephesians 6:10 AMP). Do it with an assurance ". . . that He who began a good work in you will continue until the day of Jesus Christ [right up to the time of His return], developing [that good work] and perfecting and bringing it to full completion in you" (Philippians 1:6 AMP).

To be strong in the Lord, you must first fill your head and your heart with the Scriptures. You must memorize scriptures from the Bible, by book and verse number, so you can quote them properly. As you are doing this, you are sowing into your heart seeds which the Holy Spirit can germinate. He can then bring to your remembrance from time to time that which you have stored in your spirit. It is imperative for you to be so soaked with the Word of God, so it will be ready for you to speak it out at a moment's notice.

The Word of God is spirit and life to those who receive it by faith and who choose to live by it and obey it. When you know the God of the Bible, because Jesus is the living Word, you will believe it, live it, and obey it, and it will save your soul, quicken your body, and illuminate your mind. The Word of God is full and final, infallible, reliable and up to date, and your attitude toward it must be one of unquestioned obedience. If a thing is in the Bible it is so; it is not even to be prayed about; it is to be received and acted upon because the inactivity of your faith is a robber which will steal your blessing. Your increase in faith comes by your actions, by using what you have and what you know. Your life must be one of always acting in faith. You must train yourself to obey the Word of God at all times. I Samuel 15:22 says, "To obey is better than sacrifice." Because you believe, you always act in obedience to God's Word. You must have such confidence in what the Lord said, that you would take Him at His word and act upon it, simply because He said it.

You must learn you are nothing without the Holy Spirit in your life, and you must spend quality time, completely shut in with Him every day. You must allow the Holy Spirit to talk to you and allow youself to hear and to obey His Word. You must learn to rely completely and unquestioningly on the Holy Spirit. You must spend quality time, "praying always with all prayer and supplication in the Spirit and watching thereunto with all perseverance and supplication for all saints," edifying, or building yourself up in your most holy faith (Ephesians 6:18; Jude 20).

God has a desire to have a people who are like Him, a living image of His son and He will help you achieve these goals. You only have to make the choice of daily obedience. We can see in Hebrews 4:11-16 that Holy Spirit anointed ministers are the only voices which will produce mature Christians. As a mature and holy man of God, you will follow after the Holy Spirit and not after the flesh (Ephesians 6:10 AMP; Philippians 1:6 AMP).

How much does God love you? John 3:16 tells us that He, "God so loved the world [that's you] that He gave His only begotten Son, that whosoever believeth in Him should not perish, but have everlasting life." And II Peter 1:3-9 (AMP) says that:

> His divine power has bestowed upon you all things that [are requisite and suited] to life and godliness, through the [full personal] knowledge of Him who called you by and to His own glory and excellence (virtue).
>
> By means of these He has bestowed on you His precious and exceeding great promises, so that through them you may escape [by flight] from the moral decay (rottenness and corruption) that is in the world because of covetousness (lust and greed), and become shares (partakers) of the divine nature.
>
> For this very reason, adding your diligence [to the divine promises], employ every effort in exercising your faith to develop virtue (excellence, resolution, Christian energy), and in [exercising] virtue [develop] knowledge (intelligence), And in [exercising] goodness [develop] self-control, and in [exercising] self-control [develop] steadfastness (patience, durance), and in [exercising] steadfastness [develop] godliness (piety), And in [exercising] godliness [develop] brotherly affection, and in [exercising] brotherly affection [develop] Christian love.
>
> For as these qualities are yours and increasingly abound in you, they will keep [you] from being idle or unfruitful unto the [full personal] knowledge of our Lord Jesus Christ (the Messiah, the Anointed One).
>
> For whoever lacks these qualities is blind [spiritually] shortsighted, seeing only what is near to him, and has become oblivious [to the fact] that he was cleansed from his old sins.

Where do you stand? Do you know Jesus Christ as your personal Lord and Savior? If not, I encourage you to make the following confession of faith:

"Oh God in Heaven, I believe with all of my heart that Jesus has been raised from the dead. I invite You Lord Jesus to come into my heart and be my Lord and fill me with your Holy Spirit.

I repent of all my sin and I renounce the devil and everything he stands for. I repent of the past and declare You Lord Jesus are my future. I believe it and I receive it, In Jesus Name."

(Acts 2:21, Romans 8:9 11, 10:9, John 3:5-6, 15:16, Mark 11:23).

I would not promise that after this day you will be without sorrow or that happiness will follow you every day of your life. We live in an imperfect world. I can promise you that God's life will continue to grow within you if you will let it, and that your lives together will therefore always be good. Kathy and I rejoice with you that you have found one another, that you have discovered life together, and that you have all become strong in that process of growth and discovery. God does not promise us a smooth ride, but He does promise us a gentle landing if we will stay the course with Him.

One of the greatest challenges you will encounter in your walk by faith is that most people are ignorant of God's ways of doing things. When you begin to walk by faith, you may face opposition from the people in your life. Most people believe they just have to take what comes their way and that is all that there is to life. They don't know about living by faith and the plan that God has for everything in life. They don't know God addresses the issues of life in His written Word, and gives us guidance through our born-again inner man.

When you made Jesus Christ the Lord of your life, greatness was born in your heart. But only when you discover that God has put that greatness in there will you ever achieve it. You will become what God has called you to become when you work at moving in that direction every day.

To get to the place where you totally believe and rely on the Word of God, you must start where you are and let the Lord help you. I encourage you to start each day with this confession of faith for, "as you start your day, so goes it."

"Good Morning Lord Jesus. For this day I again declare You are my Lord and I submit this day and all that it contains to you, for this is the day that the Lord has made I will rejoice and be glad in it, for the joy of the Lord is my strength and I am strong in the Lord and the power of His might and I can do all things through Christ which strengthens me. For God is working in me, creating in me the power and the desire, both to will and to work for His good pleasure.

I have been made in the God class; you Lord have placed your life in me and I am dominated by spiritual glow; and I now walk in the light of life. And the life which I now live in the flesh I live by the faith of the son of God who loved me, and gave himself for me.

I love You Lord with all my heart and with all my soul and with all of my mind and with all of my strength. And with Your help I am going to be a good Steward of Your commandment to love my neighbor as myself because that is what pleases You, for You said that "when we do those things that are pleasing in Your sight, whatever I ask in Your Name, You give it to me." In Jesus Name! (Galatians 2:20; John 1:4, 8:12; Psalm 118:24 Genesis 1:26).

Note: One of the greatest hindrances to answered prayer is not doing those things that are pleasing to God (sin) (I John 3:22).

4

THE GREAT COMMANDMENT

Master, which is the great commandment in the law?

Jesus said unto him, Thou shalt love the Lord thy God with all thy heart, and with all thy soul, and with all thy mind.

This is the first and great commandment.

And the second is like unto it, Thou shalt love thy neighbor as thyself.

On these two commandments hang all the law and the prophets"

(Matthew 22:36-40; Mark 12:29-31; Luke 10:27).

Note: The law, refers to the first five chapters of the Old Testament and "the prophets" refers to the balance of the Old Testament (Luke 16:16-17).

You are to obey the commandment as He gave it to you. You are to love the Lord your God with all your heart, with all your soul, with all your mind, and then you are to love your neighbor as you love yourself, in that order. You don't begin by trying to love your neighbor as yourself. No, you begin by loving God with all your heart whether you feel like it or not. There is nothing in the Bible about your feelings; this scripture is talking about your heart condition. But as you receive God's Word, God's love, into your heart, and allow your faith to grow and mature, then it will allow you to express your love for your neighbor.

Love and selfishness are the two greatest forces in life. Your daily choices determine whether you operate in one or the other. Love activates the law of the Spirit of life, while selfishness activates the law of sin and death (Romans 8:2).

To walk in the spirit is to allow the Holy Spirit living on the inside of you, the Word of God, to control your spirit and your life. To walk in the flesh is to allow your emotions, your outward man, to control your life. Sin and death are the result of living in the flesh, or letting your body control your life.

The commandment to love is the most important commandment of all. To love is a commandment and not an attitude, feeling, or a suggestion. Anyone who does not walk in love toward his or her neighbor does not know God because "God is love" (I John 4:7-8).

Just as God is love, Satan is selfishness (Isaiah 14:12-14). A selfish person says "I, me and my," instead of thinking of the other person first. As you gradually step out of your "selfish complaining mode" and into your "love mode" you will soon realize that you love God enough to change the things about yourself which are not pleasing to Him. You will desire to be more like Jesus. He wasn't selfish, He didn't complain, and He didn't criticize people for their mistakes. If He didn't, why should you? Determine to be more like Jesus.

Speaking negative words over your life has only brought negative results into your life. So I encourage you to take the time and learn to speak God's Word over every area of your life and achieve positive results.

Confess: Father, in Jesus Name, I love you with all of my heart, with all of my soul, with all of my mind, and with all of my strength; and I release my faith because Your Word says that I am to love You and my neighbor as I love myself. On that hangs all the law and the prophets. I choose to love my neighbor as myself because it pleases You, and Your Word says that if I do those things that are pleasing in Your sight, whatever I ask, I will receive from You. I receive your love for me today.

I encourage you to confess it over and over again. Allow it to penetrate into your memory, and stay with it. Practice it again and again until it is perfected in your life. You will always rise to the level of your confession. I John 4:12 tells us "If we love one another, God dwelleth in us, and his love is perfected in us." The more you confess it by faith, the bigger your faith will grow on the inside of you. You cannot say with your mouth, "I love the Lord my God" without your born again spirit rising up and getting bigger on the inside of you (I John 3:21-24).

Read: Matthew 22:36-40: Galatians 5:13-26: Romans 8 and the entire book of I John to learn more about God's great love that He has for you.

To know and understand this great love God has for you, you must know God, not just know about Him. As such, there is a great difference in knowing a lot about the Bible and living the Bible!

> Everything that goes into a life of pleasing God has been given to us by getting to know, personally and intimately, the One who invited us to God.
> The best invitation we will ever receive (II Peter 1:3-4 The Message Bible).

I recommend that every time you find a verse in the Bible which says something specific about God, that you underline it or make a note of it and spend time getting to really know God. It is important to know just what God will or will not do in any given situation.

5

THE KEY TO UNDERSTANDING GOD'S LOVE

In I Corinthians 13:8 (AMP) Paul says "Love never fails [never fades out or becomes obsolete or comes to an end]" and verses 12 and 13 say:

> For now we are looking in a mirror that gives only a dim (blurred) reflection [of reality as in a riddle or enigma], but then [when perfection comes] we shall see in reality and face to face! Now I know in part (imperfectly), but then I shall know and understand fully and clearly, even in the same manners as I have been fully and clearly known and understood [by God].
>
> And so faith, hope, love abide [faith—conviction and belief respecting man's relation to God and divine things; hope—joyful and confident expectation of eternal salvation; love—true affection for God and man, growing out of God's love for and in us], these three; but the greatest of these is love.

Do you really understand the depth of Gods love for you? In Ephesians 3:14-20 Paul says:

> For this cause I bow my knees unto the Father of our Lord Jesus Christ.
>
> Of whom the whole family in heaven and earth is named.

That he would grant you, according to the riches of his glory, to be strengthened with might <u>by his Spirit in the inner man</u>; <u>That Christ may dwell in your hearts</u> by faith; that you, being rooted and grounded in love, May be able to comprehend with all saints what is the breadth, the length, and depth, and height; And to know <u>the love of Christ</u>, which passeth knowledge, that you might be filled with all the fullness of God. Now unto him that is able to do exceeding abundantly above all that we ask or think, according to the power that worketh in us.

Paul is praying in Vs:16 that God "would grant you, according to the riches of his glory," or His Holy Spirit living in you to "strengthen you with might [mighty power] in your inner man," your spirit being, the real you (I Corinthians 6:17).

Is it no wonder so few people come to know and understand the God kind of love? Many people are hurt every day by people who call themselves Christians who are either ignorant or don't have an understanding of God's love. Whatever the case, they aren't allowing God's grace to shine in their lives. Man in his human nature just does not have the ability to understand God. Do you really understand God's love for you? "God is a spirit." To know God you must first have a desire to know Him; and then you must yield yourself to the Holy Spirit to be strengthened with His might in your inner man or your spirit being—the real you! His desire is to indwell your innermost being and personality. You need Christ dwelling in your heart to enable the Holy Spirit in you to teach you how to be "rooted and grounded in love." In this way, you may be able to "comprehend what is the breadth, and length, and depth, and height of the love of God which surpasses knowledge so that you might be filled with all the fullness of God." Verse 20 tells us God is the one who has the ability to do just that, through "the power that works in us"—that power, that anointing "that is able to do exceeding abundantly above all we ask or think." John 6:63 (AMP) tells us "It is the Spirit Who gives life [He is the Life-giver]; the flesh conveys no benefit whatsoever [there is no profit in it].

The words (truths) that I have been speaking to you are spirit and life" (John 8:12). Jesus said to the Apostles in John 16:7-15:

It is expedient for You that I go away: for if I go not away, the Comforter will not come unto you; but if I depart, I will send him unto you.

And when he is come, he will reprove the world of sin, and of righteousness, and of judgment:

Of sin, because they believe not on me;

Of righteousness, because I go to my Father, and you see me no more;

Of judgment, because the prince of the world is judged.

I have yet many things to say unto you, but you cannot bear them now.

Howbeit when he, the Spirit of truth, is come, he will guide you into all truth; for he shall not speak of himself; but whatsoever he shall hear, that shall he speak: and he will show you things to come.

He shall glorify me: for he shall receive of mine, and shall show it unto you.

All things that the Father hath are mine: therefore said I, that he shall take of mine, and shall show it unto you.

Now let us read this same verse from the Amplified Bible and get a more detailed understanding of what Jesus is saying to us. Pay close attention to what God is telling you here about how to get a complete understanding of God's Word! The Holy Spirit speaks to our conscience to convict us of sin and convince us of our righteousness.

However, I am telling you nothing but the truth when I say it is profitable (good, expedient, advantageous) for you that I go away. Because if I do not go away, the Comforter (counselor, Helper, advocate, Intercessor, Strengthener, standby) will not come to you [into close fellowship with you]; but if I go away, I will send Him to you [to be in close fellowship with you].

And when He comes, He will convict and convince the world and bring demonstrations to it about sin and about righteousness (uprightness of heart and right standing with God) and about judgment:

33

About sin, because they do not believe in Me [trust in, rely on, and adhere to Me];

About righteousness (uprightness of heart and right standing with God), because I go to My Father, and you will see Me no longer; About judgment, because the ruler (evil genius, prince) of this world [Satan] is judged and condemned and sentence already is passed upon him.

I have still many things to say to you, but you are not able to bear them or take them upon you or to grasp them now.

But when He, the Spirit of Truth (the Truth-giving Spirit) comes, He will guide you unto all the Truth (the whole, full Truth), For He will not speak His own message [on His own authority]; but He will tell whatever He hears [from the Father; He will give the message that has been given to Him], and He will announce and declare to you the things that are to come [that will happen in the future].

He will honor and glorify Me, because He will take of (receive, draw upon) what is Mine and will reveal (declare, disclose, transmit) it to you.

Everything that the Father has is Mine. That is what I meant when I said that He [the Spirit] will take the things that are Mine and will reveal (declare, disclose, transmit) it to you.

This is what is called revelation knowledge (Matthew 16:15-17; I Corinthians 2:9-12; Ephesians 1:17; Colossians 1:9-10). Jesus is telling us here that it is expedient for each and every one of us that He needs to go away for our benefit; for if He does not go not away the Comforter [the Holy Spirit] will not come unto us. But when He has come unto us things will begin to change. We will begin to change because the Holy Ghost is now able to deliver that "love of God" to the new sons of God and it recreates his human spirit and causes it to be reborn in Christ or reborn in love (II Corinthians 5:17; Romans 8:17-19).

Jesus told his disciples to wait for all that the Father had for them. He was referring to the power that they would receive when the Holy Spirit come upon them (Acts 10:38). We should also wait actively on God by listening to what He is telling us to do instead of running ahead and doing something in the flesh. We often have preconceived ideas about how God wants us to do things and how we should act. We have a tendency to want God's provision to come in a way that is predictable and sure, but it just doesn't always happen that way (Lamentations 3:25; Acts 1:8). God knew that we would need help understanding His plan for us, so He sent the Holy Spirit to dwell in every Christian—to be our guide, our counselor, our helper, and our comforter (John 14:16, 26, 15:26; 16:13-15)

Romans 8:26-28tells us,

> Likewise the Spirit also helpeth our infirmities [our weaknesses]: for we know not what we should pray for as we ought: but the Spirit itself maketh intercession for us with groaning which cannot be uttered.
>
> And he that searcheth the hearts knoweth what is the mind of the Spirit, because he maketh intercession for the saints according to the will of God.
>
> And we know that all things work together for good to them that love God, to them who are the called according to his purpose.

Verses 26-27 tell us God has given us the Holy Spirit to help us in our weaknesses. When we get into a situation where we simply do not know what to pray as we should, we are to let Jesus by the Holy Spirit do the praying through us.

Verse 28 is probably one of the most misquoted scriptures in the Bible. People out of ignorance use it to explain away all sorts of situations. All things do not work together for good to them that love God! To get the intent of what was said here start by reading verse 27 above, and note that the words "the will of" were added, I think, by the translators and need to be blocked out to get a correct understanding of what is being said here. ". . . because he maketh intercession for the saints according to God." Romans 8:34 tells us Jesus is setting at the right hand of God making intercession for us. Jesus is in heaven, He is our intercessor, and He knows the mind of God and knows how God would pray. We through our carnal mind do not know how God would pray, so He has come up with a way which will allow Him to intercede for us according to God, through our spirit, by the Holy Spirit that is in us, in the manner that God would pray.

In verse 28, what "all things" is he referring to here? All things that Jesus prayed through you, in the spirit, about that situation! He prayed the way that God would pray about it. He prayed God's perfect will about that situation and He said "all things" will work together for good after God has prayed about it through His Son Jesus.

Praying in tongues, praying in the spirit is one of the greatest helps God has provided for us and it is no wonder the devil fights so hard against it.

The intent of this scripture is to allow you to understand that Jesus, the intercessor who is in Heaven sitting at the right hand of the Father, is praying through the Holy Spirit who lives in your spirit, through your mouth, using your voice, praying the prayer that God would pray.

It is what you pray about in the spirit that causes things to begin to work together for your good. These are things of God, not the things of the devil. This scripture is talking about allowing God to intervene into a given situation.

Many people don't walk in the spirit, because they choose to go by their feelings. Don't listen to your feelings, because feelings are the voice of the body. Stop letting your feelings rule your life. If you determine what is right and wrong by how things feel, you will be in danger of making many wrong choices in life. You will reach true spiritual maturity by choosing to do the right thing while it still feels wrong—in other words, by choosing to turn away from things that feel right when the Bible clearly says they are wrong. You can feel wrong and still do what is right. You must train yourself to listen to God, because it is the Holy Spirit that bears witness to your spirit (I John 5:6).

We are directed in Galatians 5:16-17, to "walk in the spirit," for if you walk in the spirit, ". . . you shall not fulfill the lust of the flesh.

For the flesh lusts against the Spirit, and the Spirit against the flesh: and these are contrary the one to the other: so that you cannot do the things that you would." And John 16:13-14 (AMP) tells us:

> But when He, the Spirit of Truth (the Truth-giving Spirit) comes, He will guide you into all the Truth (the whole, full Truth). For He will not speak His own message [on His own authority]; but He will tell whatever He hears [from the Father; He will give the message that has been given to Him], and He will announce and declare to you the things that are to come [that will happen in the future].

He will honor and glorify Me, because He will take or (receive, draw upon) what is Mine and will reveal (declare, disclose, transmit it to you. <u>Everything that the Father has is Mine</u>. That is what I meant when I said <u>He [the Spirit] will take the things that are Mine and will reveal (declare, disclose, transmit) it to you.</u>

How important is this to you? Do you want all that God has for you? Remember, it is your choice!

God is a spirit, and you are a spirit being. God contacts you, leads you, and deals with you through your spirit. He does not communicate with you directly through your mind, because the Holy Spirit does not dwell in your soul or body but in your spirit.

When you are praying in the spirit, guidance comes up from the inside of you because your spirit is active and in contact with God but your mind is not, for it is through your spirit that God gives you guidance.

The devil is a flesh devil and he communicates with you through your mind, so it is imperative to you that you learn to differentiate or tell the difference between what you are hearing from your spirit and that what comes from your mind.

While you are praying in the spirit, you will at times experience from down deep inside of you the knowing, knowledge or understanding of what God wants to tell you, or receive directions from Him. This will rise up on the inside of you to take shape in the form of a thought that you won't always be able to put into words, because your understanding, which has nothing to do with it, is a function of your soul, not of your spirit, but you will know exactly [on the inside of you] what God is saying to you and what direction you are to take.

God is faithful to always lead or guide us in the direction He wants us to go. Romans 8:14 tells us: "For as many as are led by the Spirit of God, they are the sons of God." And how does He lead us? Verse 16 tells us, "the spirit itself beareth witness with our spirit." Notice God's spirit bears witness with our spirit or testifies together with our spirit. God's spirit dwells in us, and God uses His Spirit which lives in us, that "inward witness," to lead or guide us, and the Spirit of God that is in us will also "quicken or make alive [restore to life] our mortal bodies" (Romans 8:11).

When you get to the place where you hear God's voice, you listen to it, and act on it, it is then when you will really live. The more you get to know the Lord, and get into His Word, the greater becomes your perception of His voice in your heart. As you hear the prompting of the Holy Spirit, to pray for those around you, or how to act in a specific situation, don't dismiss it, but begin to listen to what God is saying to you, because you never know when it might directly affect those you hold near and dear or someone you may have never met (Hebrews 4:3).

> It is the spirit who gives life [He is the Life-giver]; the flesh conveys no benefit whatever [there is no profit in it].

And James 2:26 tells us

> ". . . the body without the spirit is dead (John 6:63 AMP).

Now that you have a grip of what the Holy Spirit wants to do in your life, you need to know that the Holy Spirit was implanted into your reborn spirit when you asked Jesus Christ into your heart as your Lord and Savior, but He will not do anything without your permission (Romans 10:9-10; Colossians 2:9; I John 4:15).

You are free to be a child of the Most High God. He has breathed His very life into you, and you have His royal blood flowing in your veins. God saw you before you were ever formed in your mother's womb. He knew you and planned out your life before you were born. You are a person of divine destiny. You are a one-of-a-kind part of God's creation, put here to do what He put you here to do. You have a God given assignment, something only you can accomplish. You are an original, and God has accepted and approved of you. But it takes steps of faith to stay in God's plan. He is a faith God, and He expects you to walk by faith to accomplish your God-given assignment. Remember, God has a plan for you and it is a good plan, an uncommon plan, it is not an average mediocre plan, but a great plan. So step up and seek out that plan and cooperate with God so it will be wonderfully fulfilled in your life (Proverbs 3:5-8, 20:5; John 15:16; Ephesians 1:4; I Peter 2:9).

There is a difference between the Holy Spirit being "with you" and "in you" (John 14:17). The Spirit "with you," the new birth, is a well of water in you, springing up into everlasting life, and that water in this well is for one purpose, and that is to bless you.

The Spirit "in you" is the infilling of the Holy Spirit which delivers, not just one, but rivers of living water flowing out of you which will bring the anointing [the power of God] enabling you to be a blessing to others.

The promise of receiving the Holy Spirit is for everyone in the Body of Christ because God gave His Spirit to the Church on the Day of Pentecost (Acts 2:33, 39). As a partaker of your covenant with God, however, you must individually receive what He has given to you. When you ask for the indwelling of the Holy Spirit, the Word of God promises you that you shall receive.

> And I say unto you, Ask, and it shall be given you; seek, and you shall find; knock, and it shall be opened unto you.
>
> For every one that asketh receiveth; and he that seeketh findeth; and to him that knocketh it shall be opened.
>
> If a son shall ask bread of any of you that is a father, will he give him a stone? Or if he ask a fish, will he for a fish give him a serpent?
>
> Or if he shall ask an egg, will he offer him a scorpion?
>
> If you then, being evil, know how to give good gifts unto your children: how much more shall your heavenly Father give the Holy Spirit to them that ask him? (Luke 11:9-13).

Acts 2:4 tells us when the believers received the Holy Ghost they began to speak with other tongues. "And they were all filled with the Holy Ghost and began to speak with other tongues, as the Spirit gave them utterance." This is still true today. When you accept the Spirit's indwelling, your spirit will immediately have a desire to express itself in praise to God. The Holy Spirit will give utterance through you as you give Him permission to do so. He will not do it without your permission!

When you pray in the tongues, you are praying in the spirit. You are letting the Holy Spirit pray through your spirit. I Corinthians 14:14 (AMP) says, "My spirit [by the Holy Spirit within me] prays . . . ." Just as English is the voice of your mind, your prayer language is the voice of your spirit.

To receive the infilling of the Holy Spirit simply say: "Father, I am a new creature in Christ. Fill me with Your Holy Spirit to enable me to be a powerful witness of Jesus. I believe that I receive the Holy Spirit just as the disciples did on the Day of Pentecost" (II Corinthians 5:17; John 7:37-39; Galatians 3:14 & 29; Mark 11:24).

The Holy Ghost actually came on you to deliver God to you. God is love, and if the love of God has been shed abroad in your heart by the Holy Ghost (Romans 5:5, 8:11), then that same God who is love has been shed abroad in your heart by that same Holy Ghost. When the Holy Ghost showed up, it was to carry to every believer a dose or injection of the love of God. When you invited Jesus into your heart as your Lord and savior, you were filled up with God who is love and this love is operating on the inside of you (2 Corinthians 5:17-19; Ephesians 2:10; 6:17).

> Know ye that your body is the temple of the Holy Ghost which is in you, which ye have of God, and ye are not your own?
> For ye are bought with a price: <u>therefore glorify God</u> [honor God and bring glory to Him] <u>in your body and in your spirit</u>, which are God's (I Corinthians 6:19-20).

How do we do that? You, "Submit yourself therefore to God," or be subject to God (James 4:7).

Did you notice what God is directing you to do here? You have a choice to continue being your same old self or stepping up and putting out the effort to be the new self God has chosen you to be. Jesus came to set you free (John 10:10), but it is up to you to decide how far you want to go in those "heavenly" ways of thinking, talking, and living. II Timothy 1:6 tells us "you are to stir up the gift of God, which is in you." If you choose to do so, begin to pray, "Lord, I stir myself up to be ready to be used as an end-time servant to open my mouth and declare the wonderful works of God. I choose to live my life to be a blessing to others. So help me ready myself for Your service. Your perfect will be done in me and in my life and ministry." In Jesus Name.

It is your choice: nobody can do it for you! You are in charge of your destiny, and God will back you with all the powers of heaven! You must ask yourself, what am I doing with the life of God that has been freely given to me? Do I reject it because I don't think I am valuable enough to be loved? Do I believe God is like other people who have rejected and hurt me? Or do I receive His love by faith, believing He is greater than my failures and weaknesses?

The Truth, God's Word, is one of the most powerful weapons a believer has against the kingdom of darkness. Truth is light, and the Bible says the darkness has never overpowered the light and it never will. God's Word is the final authority, and you can choose to live by it, or reject it, but whichever you choose, it will never fade away. So, choose to walk in the light of life! (John 8:12, 15:26, 16:13-14; Romans 8:26-27; I Corinthians 2:9-16; Ephesians 5:2).

I am sure you have heard God speak to you, and you have asked yourself, was that God, or was it just my mind playing tricks on me. I have learned through experience that God is always talking to me through the Holy Spirit, but I have to sadly admit I haven't always listened to what He was saying and have missed out on a lot of important things not only in my personal life but the lives of those around me.

I had a business where I went out and made repairs to other people's equipment. When I received a call and left the house to go to the garage to get my truck, I would often hear the Holy Spirit instruct me to take along different items, only to get out to the job and have a need for that item. The times I did not listen to and act upon God's directions, I often had to return home and get them or have somebody bring the items out to the job site.

This book is the end result of my listening to God. What He has done for me, He will also do it for you, because God is no respecter of persons. If you will allow Him, He will guide you in every area of your life, whether it is physically, financially, socially, spiritually, or mentally. The key is your willingness to surrender those areas of your life totally to God (Acts 10:34).

God doesn't cast His pearls before swine, and as such, He has purposely arranged it so His Word can only be understood by revelation. The Bible says He has hidden that wisdom for you, not from you. This is why Jesus said in Luke 12:2, ". . . there is nothing covered that it shall not be revealed; neither hid, but what it shall be known" (Matthew 7:6; Colossians 2:3; Proverbs 14:6).

God will never just drop great revelations into you lap while you are just doing your own thing. Jesus said, "If any man have ears to hear, let him hear" (Mark 4:23). God has given you inner ears to hear His Spirit with. But you are responsible for the hearing. You are now responsible for seeking out this revelation knowledge, revelation which can come only from God (Matthew 16:15-17; John 3:27; I Corinthians 2:10).

The revelation of God's Word comes to us through our spirit. It comes to us from the inside out. Before our mind can fully take hold of it and start rejoicing over it, the Word has to become strong enough in us to overcome the outward evidence to the contrary, and take over our entire being.

For this to happen, we must meditate on the Word of God. We must feed on it and stir ourselves up on purpose with the truth of it. We must spend quality time developing our faith (Joshua 1:8).

God isn't doling out revelations one here and another there. He sent the Holy Spirit who has all the revelations in Him. When you get yourself into a position to receive by meditating the Word, praying, and fellowshipping with the Lord, then and only then will you begin to receive those revelations from Him. So it's on your end that the responsibility now lies (John 16:13-15).

Peter tells us grace and peace are multiplied to us through the knowledge of God and of Jesus our Lord (II Peter 1:2). The Greek word knowledge, *epignoosis* means, precise or correct knowledge or exact knowledge revealed in such a way that it's not hindered by the physical sense or by someone's ability to communicate.

Did you notice you need knowledge both of God and of Jesus? You need to know Almighty God as your very own Father and Jesus as your Lord and Savior. You need more than a mental understanding of it. You need to know it on the inside of you and this kind of knowing comes only by revelation.

John 10:10 (AMP) gives us a guideline which will enable you to determine if you are hearing from God or from some other source. "The thief comes only in order to steal and kill and destroy. I came that they may have and enjoy life, and have it in abundance (to the full, till it overflows)." Notice Jesus is the deliver and Satan is the oppressor.

Stop and think, anytime you are in doubt about what you are hearing in your spirit. If I do this, will it cause me to lose something or be harmful to me, my loved ones, my friends or neighbors or will it bring peace and tranquility and advance my enjoyment of life to its fullest. Will it bring peace and tranquility or will it bring fear and torment? The devil will tell you that you can't do that, you're not smart enough, you don't have the right skills, that it is too complicated, etc. But God will always tell you, "If you can believe, all things are possible to those who believe" (Mark 9:23). So, always use the Word of God as your final authority when making these decisions:

> The Word that God speaks is alive and full of power [making
> it active, operative, energizing, and effective]; it is sharper
> than any two-edged sword, penetrating to the dividing line
> of the breadth of life (soul) and [the immortal] spirit, and
> of joints and marrow [of the deepest parts of our nature],

exposing and sifting and analyzing and judging the very
thoughts and purposes of the heart (Hebrews 4:12 AMP).

Remember, the Word of God has within itself the power to do what it says, but it takes action on your part to make it happen! If you want to walk through trouble into victory, you will have to intensely focus your attention on the Word of God. You will have to be like the righteous man in Psalm 112:7 who is not afraid of evil tidings because "his heart is fixed, trusting in the Lord."

You can start by confessing every day from Psalm 91:1-2, "I am he that dwelleth in the secret place of the most High, and I abide under the shadow of the Almighty. And I say of you Lord, You are my refuge, You are my fortress, You are my God, and in You do I place my trust." As you do this you only need to read verses 5 through 16 and see the blessings of God that you will reap when you put your trust in Him.

At times you will have to be a little rough on yourself when you catch yourself getting distracted and your thoughts wandering. You will have to tell your mind to, "get back onto the things of God, "which is how you "crucify your flesh" to bring it back under the dominion of your spirit where it belongs. You will find your flesh won't like it and the devil won't either. He will try to get you to let your mind wander or draw your attention to other things and before you know it your mind is on something other than God and His Word. If you will let him, the devil will continually plant seeds of distraction into your life, and they will grow up to become attitudes and habits such as negative thoughts which will keep you from receiving what God has for you.

There are three things you need to learn and adopt into your life.

1. Pay attention to, and spend quality time listening to what God is instructing you to do. You have to purposely pay attention to Him, and you should expect to get something from Him such as divine revelation.

When you have a major decision to make, you can't just look at the world around you. You must consult with God and recognize His hand on your life. God can steer you away from situations that seem good on the surface but are designed by the devil to steal away God's best plan for your life.

2. Fear not, because fear is the source of all unbelief. Fear connects you to the spirit of death and faith connects you to the spirit of life. The spiritual

force of fear is working all of the time, challenging everything God says. Struggling to believe God's Word is a serious sign of fear's presence.

II Timothy 1:7 tells us: "For God hath not given us the spirit of fear; but of power, and of love, and of a sound mind." Notice, there is a difference between the spirit of fear, the Spirit of Power, the Spirit of Love, and the Spirit of a sound mind. A mind under the influence of fear is not a sound mind and it is not from God. There is a difference between the spirit of fear and the emotion called fear. Everybody needs to know how they interact and how they work because if you confuse them you can put yourself into a state of confusion and worry. God's Word tells us many times to "fear not." If you don't learn to conquer fear, it will conquer you (Isaiah 41:10). There is an emotion of fear that is God-given to help you, and there is the spirit of fear. The latter fear is made up of phobias, which come from the devil. These are two entirely different kinds of fear, and they serve two entirely different purposes.

We all need to know how to bridle the emotion of fear and learn how to allow it to help us master our moods and help us accomplish our mission. Healthy fear is an asset to life and all that we are to accomplish.

The spirit of fear comes from Satan, the prince of darkness. When you choose to live in darkness, Satan has the authority to run your life. And when you reject darkness and choose to live in the light, as Christ is in the light, you have the joy of following the light of the world. It's your choice whether you live in the kingdom of light or the kingdom of darkness. You either choose Jesus or Satan to be your master (Deuteronomy 30:19).

The spirit of fear comes into your life by sin and is sustained by sin and like a virus, it will invade your soul and will require more evil in which it might live. Sin gives fear a license to rule your life. Fear attacks your mind, telling you that you are too tired to try again, you are too weak to win, and you are too exhausted to endure.

To overcome the spirit of fear, you need to take charge of your life and confess you are a child of God, an ambassador of the Lord Jesus Christ to the kingdom of God. And last but not least you need to think like it, act like it, and live like it. If you will stand on the Word of God your faith will tell you:

> You are more than conquerors through Christ. Nothing is impossible with God. For they that wait upon the Lord shall renew their strength, they shall mount up on wings as eagles,

they shall run and not grow weary, they shall walk and they shall not faint, so, fear not, for God is with you" (Romans 8:37; Luke 1:37; Isaiah 40:31; John 14:18; Luke 12:32).

Romans 8:2 tells us, ". . . the law of the Spirit of life in Christ Jesus has made me free from the law of sin and death." It is easy to see that the spirit of fear can in no way be a part of the Law of the Spirit of Life in Christ Jesus, because there is no fear in Christ Jesus. In fact, just the opposite is true. The Law of Christ Jesus is the Law of Love, and perfect love casts out fear. I John 4:18 tells us "There is no fear in love; but perfect love casteth out fear: because fear hath torment. He that feareth is not made perfect in love."

3. Stand up and act like you are a believer or a child of God.

Don't be spiritually weak and quit in the face of a little persecution from the devil. You have the God-given authority to submit yourself to God, to resist the devil and then and only then will he flee from you, as if in terror (James 4:7).

God is always speaking to us. He is giving us the instructions we need and He is giving us the wisdom we need to live as conquerors.

God is a spirit and He communicates to us, spirit to spirit. God talks to us through our spirit, and if you know Jesus Christ as your personal Lord and Savior you can hear the voice of the Lord! You can visit and talk with Him all the time. That is part of your righteousness. Jesus took your sin and gave you His robe of righteousness, or your right standing with God. He has become so totally one with you that He has given you the authority to use His Name. In other words, God sees you and will deal with you as though you had never sinned. You are the righteousness of God, and the Blood of Jesus has cleanses you from all sin—all unrighteousness, if and when you believe God. If you choose to accept your righteousness, God will never take His eyes off you.

To be righteous is to be reconciled to right standing. Righteousness is a covenant word meaning being made right, or to be reconciled to right standing. In I John 1:9 it simply means your sins have been blotted out or removed (Job 36:7-9; Isaiah 32:17, 43:25).

God will honor you, lavish and promote you endlessly, and when things are bad, when afflictions and suffering comes on you, He will tell you where you have gone wrong and what you need to do to correct things (Hebrews 11:6).

What are you believing God for? Don't just say it, confess it. Get scriptures that pertain to what you are believing God for and stand on them. Speak them out several times every day and let the Word come out of your mouth in faith and in power. "For faith commeth by hearing and hearing by the Word of God." And you activate that faith by saying what God has to say about you and about the situation in His Word (Romans 4:17, 10:17).

Your faith is the key; faith brings to pass the things you are hoping for. Faith releases God and it allows Him to work in your life.

Praying in the spirit is one of the keys to the Kingdom of God which allows you as a believer to understand the profound wisdom of God and allows you to pray the perfect will of God (Romans 8:26). When you received the Holy Spirit, you received the ability of God. Acts 1:8 tells us, "But you shall receive power, after that the Holy Ghost is come upon you: and you shall be witness unto me both in Jerusalem, and in all Judaea, and in Samaria, and unto the uttermost part of the earth." This word "power" from the Greek *dunamis* means ability, efficiency, and might. It is through the energizing force of the Holy Spirit living in you which causes you to be transformed into an effective witness for Jesus Christ. There is nothing Jesus did that you cannot do, because praying in the spirit makes great power available to you (John 14:12). Praying in the spirit is part of your spiritual armor, which allows you to experience a personal relationship with the Father. For praying in the spirit is simply your spirit interacting directly with God's Spirit. Praying in tongues is to enhance the Anointing in and upon your life; it is part of the Anointing. It edifies or builds you up spiritually and makes it easier to hear what the Holy Spirit is saying to you by putting you in contact with the deep things of God. It also allows you to pray God's perfect will when you are interceding for others. It's what strengthens and intensifies your personal relationship with God. It's God who lives on the inside of you who does the work, you are just the mouth piece! (Ephesians 6:18; Romans 8:26-27; Mark16:17; I Corinthians 2:10; 14:4, 14; Jude 20-21).

Praying in the spirit accomplishes the same thing for your spirit that eating three meals a day does for your body—it builds you up (Jude 20). Looking at it in this perspective, you can see where it is important for you to spend a few minutes praying in the spirit several times a day. Just as it is important to feed your body more than once a day, it is important to feed your spirit more than once a day.

Romans 8:16 tells us "the Spirit itself beareth witness with our spirit, assuring us that we are the children of God." Notice, God's spirit "beareth witness or testifies together with our spirit." God's Spirit dwells in us, and God uses His Spirit which lives in us, this "inward witness" to lead or guide us, and the Spirit of God that is in us will also "quicken or make alive [restore to life] our mortal bodies" (Romans 8:11). The Holy Spirit which lives in us is what gives us access to the Father; He gives us boldness and confidence and strengthens us with might.

I Thessalonians 5:19 tells us to "Quench not the spirit." To quench the spirit is to suppress or subdue, extinguish, put or shut out, look with contempt upon the gifts and or not allow the gifts to function or be used in the body. Mark 3:29 (AMP) tells us, "But whoever speaks abusively against or maliciously misrepresents the Holy Spirit can never get forgiveness, but is guilty of and is in the grasp of an everlasting trespass." Now to "speak abusively or blaspheme" is to take that which is sacred or holy and speak evil of it, to attribute to Satan the things of God (Matthew 12:31).

If you desire the infilling of the Holy Spirit of if you are not sure whether you have received it, pray this prayer;

"Father, I am a new creature in Christ. Fill me with Your Holy Spirit to enable me to be a powerful witness for Jesus. I believe that I receive the Holy Spirit just as the disciples did on the Day of Pentecost, in Jesus Name."

Now yield your voice to the Holy Spirit to pray the perfect will of God in your life. Open your mouth and just say what comes out.

The key to knowing you are praying in the spirit is that your mind is free to think about other things while your mouth is speaking out the words from the Holy Spirit.

6

THE NEW YOU

If any person is [engrafted] in Christ (the Messiah) he is a new creation (a new creature altogether); the old [previous moral and spiritual condition] has passed away. Behold the fresh and new has come!" But all things are from God, Who through Jesus Christ reconciled us to Himself [received us into favor, brought us into harmony with Himself] and gave to us the ministry of reconciliation [that by word and deed we might aim to bring others into harmony with Him].

It was God [personally present] in Christ, reconciling and restoring the world to favor with Himself, not counting up and holding against [men] their trespasses [but canceling them], and committing to us the message of reconciliation (of the restoration to favor).

So we are Christ's ambassadors, God making His appeal as it were through us. We [as Christ's personal representatives] beg you for His sake to lay hold of the divine favor [now offered you] and be reconciled to God.

For our sake He made Christ [virtually] to be sin Who knew no sin, so that in and through Him we might become [endued with, viewed as being in, and examples of] the righteousness of God [what we ought to be, approved and acceptable in right relationship with Him, by His goodness] (II Corinthians 5:17-21 AMP).

When a person comes to Christ, he receives the remission of his sins provided for him when Jesus suffered and died on the cross of Calvary. That is, his sins are blotted out. Not only were his sins blotted out, but his past life, that old sin nature has been blotted out as well. As far as God is concerned, nothing in your life prior to the moment you became born again is counted, or held against you. You were also reconciled or brought into divine favor, and accepted to become God's friend again, and have a relationship with him like Adam experienced before the fall.

Stop and think about what you have just read; you are no longer just an old sinner saved by grace, but you are a new creation in Christ Jesus. "Old things are passed away; behold all things are become new." You have been recreated "In Christ," you are a new creation; that old moral and spiritual condition is gone and God expects you to start acting like it! God has given you a new start in life, and you need only to take what God has provided for you and go with it! God has not only cleaned your slate but has provided a way for you to get back into His grace when you get out of favor with Him (I John 1:9).

"In Him or In Christ," makes you worthy to receive from God and defines just who and what you are. Every born-again believer has the life of God, the nature of God, the God-kind of life in Him. You have that life of God, His glory in you. God is love and has given you the ability to put His power to work. That is how God works through you and me. God is not here on this earth in person, but He is in us by His spirit and where the Spirit is there is liberty (I Corinthians 3:16; II Corinthians 3:17).

> Everything that goes into a life of pleasing God has been miraculously given to us <u>by getting to know, personally and intimately, the One who invited us to God.</u> The best invitation we ever received!
>
> We were also given absolutely terrific promises to pass on to you—your tickets to participation in the life of God after you turned your back on a world corrupted by lust.
>
> So don't lose a minute in building on what you've been given, complementing your basic faith with good character, spiritual understanding, alert discipline, passionate patience, reverent wonder, warm friendliness, and generous love, each dimension fitting into and developing others. With these qualities active and growing in your life, no grass will grow under your feet; no day will pass without its reward as you mature in your experience of our Master Jesus. Without

these qualities you can't see what's right before you, oblivious that your old sinful life has been wiped off the books.

So, friends, confirm God's invitation to you, his choice of you. Don't put it off; do it now. Do this, and you'll have your life on a firm footing, the streets paved and the way wide open into the eternal kingdom of our Master and Savior, Jesus Christ (II Peter 1:3-8 The Message Bible).

That if thou shalt confess with thy mouth the Lord Jesus, and shalt believe in thine heart that God hath raised him from the dead, thou shalt be saved.

For with the heart man believeth unto righteousness; and with the mouth confession is made unto salvation (Romans 10:9-10).

For some, the need to confess Jesus as lord over and over will be necessary to get to the point where they believe it in their heart. For faith in God comes by hearing the Word of God (Romans 10:17). See the confession of faith at the end of this chapter.

We were all servants or subjects of Satan, the enemy of God, until we accepted Jesus Christ as our Lord and savior. When we invited Jesus into our hearts we changed allegiance from the devil to Almighty God. And at this time in our life we are supposed to make an absolute, unconditional break with our old master because the Word of God teaches us we must make some big changes in our lives by putting off our old ways of acting, talking, and thinking, and allow Jesus is to be the new Lord, or ruler of our intellectual life as well as our heart, or spiritual life (Colossians 3:1-17).

You can't have Jesus as your savior and not as your Lord. "Therefore we are buried with him by baptism into death: that like Christ was raised up from the dead by the glory of the Father, even so we also should walk in newness of life" (Romans 6:4).

Many people want Jesus as their Savior but also want to keep Satan as their Lord. They are not willing to turn loose of their old life. They want to straddle the fence. They want the blessings of God, but they also want to keep enjoying the old sinful pleasures of the world. And they just can't figure out why God is not blessing them! But Matthew 6:24 tells us we "cannot serve two masters: for either we will hate the one, and love the other; or else we will hold to the one, and despise the other. You cannot serve God and mammon" (Luke 16:13; James 4:4; I John 2:15-17). This is why we see so many good people come to Christ and then slowly fall back into their old habits and lifestyle!

In I John 2:15-17 we are directed to:

> Love not the world, neither the things of the world. If any man love the world, the love of the Father is not in him.
>
> For all that is in the world, the lust of the flesh, and the lust of the eyes, and the pride of life, is not of the Father, but is of the world.
>
> And the world passeth away, and the lust thereof: but that doeth the will of God abideth for ever.

When you made Jesus your Lord, you gave Him say-so over your life and how it should be lived, what your eyes are allowed to see, what your ears are allowed to hear, whom you hang out with, where you work, your home and family, your vocation in life, your finances, how you make your money and how you spend it and where you live—virtually every aspect of your life. Why? Because it is His desire for you to be blessed and not cursed, but it is your choice! Most Christians never experience God's best in their lives because they don't understand how that can be accomplished (Deuteronomy 30:15-19).

> For there are three that bear record in heaven, the Father, the Word, and the Holy Ghost: and these three are one (I John 5:7).
>
> In the beginning was the Word, and the Word was with God, and the Word was God (John 1:1).
>
> And the Word was made flesh, and dwelt among us . . . (John 1:14).

Jesus is the Living Word, and God has given us the written Word to unveil the Living Word to us, and we are to give the Word of God, primarily the New Testament, first place in our lives. And by doing so, we are putting Jesus in first place. By letting the Word of God govern your life, letting the Word be the Lord of your life, by letting the Word dominate you, you are allowing Jesus to be the lord over you because Jesus and His Word are one.

So, let the Word of God, His written Word be the guide over your life. When you do, you are making Jesus the Lord over your life.

> All scripture is given by inspiration of God, and is profitable for doctrine, for reproof, for correction, for instruction in righteousness,
> That the man of God may be complete, thoroughly equipped for every good work (I Timothy 3:16-17 NKJV).

This is why a good understanding of the scriptures is far more valuable than a good education, it thoroughly equips you for every good work (Proverbs 20-23). God tells us in Hosea 4:6 "My people are destroyed for lack of knowledge." Understand, the devil and his crowd does not want you to know how much God loves you; that Jesus is alive; that He is the brightness of God's glory; that He is the express image of His person; that His Word is alive; and that you are what and who you are because you are a new creature in Christ Jesus. They do not want you to know that faith is the doorway to abundance; that it is one thing to have faith and another thing to use it; that faith is a lifestyle and it is the key to unlimited treasure. Its laws of operation are sure, steadfast, and as unchanging as Jesus Himself.

In giving Himself to us, He has given us His faith. Not just a portion of it, but all of it. He did not give us only a portion of Himself; but everything that He has and is has been given to us in a full and overflowing measure. Jesus tells us in John 10:10 that He came that we might have life, and that we might have it more abundantly. Ask yourself, am I living the abundant life? If not, why not? (Galatians 2:20; Colossians 2:10; Hebrews 11:3, 13:8; James 2:17).

The morning Jesus came out of the tomb, two men in shining garments spoke to the women who had come to place spices and ointments on His body and said, "Why seek ye the living among the dead? He is not here, but is risen" (Luke 24:5-6). This should also be telling us to not be looking for Jesus among the dead, lifeless religions of the world, but to be looking for Him where the action is: among born-again, spirit filled saints who are out saving the lost, healing the sick, and raising the dead. Mark 16:17-18 tells us the signs we should be looking for in a good Christian Church and if they are not there we should be looking elsewhere!

Jesus is alive and His Word is alive. Hebrews 4:12 tells us, "For the Word of God is quick, and powerful, and sharper than any two-edged sword, piercing even to the dividing asunder of soul and spirit, and of the joints and marrow, and is a discerner of the thoughts and intents of the heart." That same supernatural power which raised Jesus from Hell and death is in His Word. In fact, the Word of God is what raised Him up. The first chapter of Hebrews, Verse 6, is a word-for-word account of what the Father said when He brought Jesus out of the fiery pits of Hell. "And again, when he bringeth in the first begotten into the world, he saith, and let all the angels of God worship him." He had regained His place of authority and majesty with the Father. (Read all of Hebrews 1, taking special note of verse 3 and all of I Corinthians 15).

Why is that so important? Because Jesus is the Word made flesh and because you were: "born again, not of corruptible seed, but of incorruptible, by the word of God which lives and abides forever" (I Peter 1:23). You were brought forth from death in trespass and sin by the Word of His power, the Word of God which lives and abides forever, and you were:

> Buried with him in baptism, wherein also you are risen with him through the faith of the operation of God, who hath raised him from the dead.
> And you, being dead in your sins and the uncircumcision of your flesh, hath he quickened together with him, having forgiven you all trespasses:
> Blotting out the handwriting of ordinances that was against us, which was contrary to us, and took it out of the way, nailing it to the cross (Colossians 3:12:13; John 1:1; I Peter 1:23; Colossians 1:14, 2:12; Ephesians 2:5-6).

We are speaking of spiritual things here and you are just as alive as He is. His life is living in you now. Not after you get to heaven, but right now! This is what the Holy Spirit is telling us in I John 4:17: ". . . as he is, so are we in this world." Not later, but right now! We are the sons of the living God (John 1:12; Romans 8:16-17; Galatians 4:7).

I John 5:1 tells, "Whosoever believeth that Jesus is the Christ is born of God." And I John 5:4-5 tells us, "For whatsoever is born of God overcometh the world: and this is the victory that overcometh the world, even our faith. Who is he that overcometh the world, but he that believeth that Jesus is the Son of God?" Overcoming the world is our God given ability to put off that old man and put on the new man, which is renewed in knowledge after the image of him who created him (Genesis 1:26; Colossians 3:10). We are able to do this by renewing our mind with the Word of God and the instant anything contrary to God's Word comes into our life we attack it by confessing God's promises to us and over that situation.

The key is to turn off the TV, turn off the radio, turn off the world and turn on the Word of God. Spend time reading the Word several times a day, get the Word on CD and play it throughout the day when you can, play it at night while you sleep, write out verses on cards or sticky notes and place them up around the house or at work, where you can read them aloud and spend time meditating on them. Get teaching tapes from good faith based ministries and listen to them every chance you get. Remember, faith in God comes by hearing the Word of God over and over and over again; and God's desire is that you who have received Christ Jesus as Lord would walk In Him by faith (Romans 10:17; Colossians 2:6).

Jesus is alive. His Word is alive and In Him we are alive. That means His faith, which has become our faith, is alive (Galatians 2:20). In fact, His faith is in His Word, according to Romans 10:17. His faith is a living force. His faith, His hope, His love, all three are alive in us, ready to do the same works they did when He was here on the earth in His human body. And in John 14:12, Jesus said, "He that believeth on me, the works that I do shall he do also; and greater works than these shall he do; because I go to my father."

You are probably asking, how is that possible? In John 17:20-26 (AMP), Jesus is praying to The Father for the church:

> Neither for these alone do I pray [it is not for their sake only that I make this request], but also for those who will overcome to believe in (trust in, cling to, rely on) me through their word and teaching.
>
> That they all may be one, [just] as You, Father, are in Me and I in You, that they also may be one in Us, so that the world may believe and be convinced that You have sent Me.
>
> I have given to them the glory and honor which You have given Me, that they may be one [even] as We are one:
>
> I in them and You in Me, in order that they may become one and perfectly united, that the world may know and [definitely] recognize that You sent Me and that You have loved them [even] as You have loved Me.

Father, I desire that they also whom You have entrusted to Me [as Your gift to Me] may be with Me where I am, so that they may see My glory, which You have given Me [Your love gift to Me]: for You loved Me before the foundation of the world.

O just and righteous Father, although the world has not known You and has failed to recognize You and has never acknowledged You, I have known You [continually]; and these men understand and know that You have sent Me.

I have made Your Name known to them and revealed Your character and Your very Self, and I will continue to make [You] known, that the love which You have bestowed upon Me <u>may be in them</u> [felt in their hearts] and that I [Myself] <u>may be in them</u>.

Understand, the world as a whole just does not know God or the great love He has for us. They do not understand the concept of The Father, Jesus, and the Holy Spirit being in us, (verse 23) and using us to minister the gospel to them. In Matthew 28:18-20 (AMP) Jesus is telling us:

All authority (all power of rule) in heaven and on earth has been given unto me.

Go then and make disciples of all the nations, baptizing them into the name of the Father and of the Son and of the Holy Spirit.

Teaching them to observe everything that I have commanded you, and behold I am with you all the days (perpetually, uniformly, and on every occasion), to the [very] close and consummation of the age.

God has given us the power of attorney to use the Name of Jesus! And that Name has authority in this earth. The use of that Name (Jesus) is not a matter of faith, but it is a matter of assuming our legal rights in Christ, taking our place as a son of God, and using what belongs to us!

We have a right to use the Name of Jesus against our enemies, in our praise and worship and in petitions to the Father because that Name belongs to us. It has been given to us so that we might carry out the will of God and do His work here in this earth (Philippians 2:10-11).

Jesus' Name now takes the place of Jesus here upon this earth. All that Jesus could do during His earthly ministry can now be done by every believer. Jesus is in that name. All that Jesus was, all that He did, all that He is, and all that He will ever be is in that Name now and it is ours to use! (John 14:12).

When we use the Name of Jesus, we bring onto the scene the fullness of His finished work at Calvary. By our use of that Name, the living, healing Christ is present to give glory and honor to God the Father (John 24:13).

Notice, Jesus has told us to take that power and go into the world! Well, just where did Jesus get that Power? In Acts 10:38 (AMP) we learn that:

> God anointed and consecrated Jesus of Nazareth with the [Holy] Spirit and with strength and ability and power, how He went about doing good and, in particular, curing all who were harassed and oppressed by [the power of] the devil, for God was with Him.

And in Luke 4:18-19 Jesus tells us:

> The Spirit of the Lord is upon me, because he hath anointed me to preach the gospel to the poor; he hath sent me to heal the brokenhearted, to preach deliverance to the captives, and recovering of sight to the blind, to set at liberty them that are bruised, To preach the acceptable year of the Lord.

Did you notice sickness comes from being harassed and oppressed by the power of the devil, and that Jesus was anointed with the strength, ability and power to cure those sicknesses? And where does Jesus reside today? Ephesians 1:17, 20; 2:6 tells us:

> The God of our Lord Jesus Christ, the Father of glory, raised him from the dead and set him at his own right hand in the heavenly places and has also raised us up together, and made us sit together in heavenly places in Christ Jesus.

We are talking about our being "In Christ" here, with the fullness of the Godhead in us. We are talking about spiritual things. Remember, when God looks at you now, He sees you through the shed blood of Jesus (Colossians 2:9; Galatians 2:20; Isaiah 10:27).

Now that life of God in us is what allows us to:

> Go into all the world, and preach the gospel to every creature.
> He that believeth and is baptized shall be saved; but he that
> believeth not shall be dammed.
>   And these signs shall follow them that believe;
>   In my [Jesus] name shall they cast out devils; they shall
> speak with new tongues;
>   They shall take up serpents; and if they drink any deadly
> thing, it shall not hurt them; they shall lay hands on the
> sick, <u>and they shall recover</u> (Mark 16:16-18).

"These signs shall follow them that believe" (Mark 16:17). What is it to believe? It is to have such confidence in what the Lord said that we would take Him at His word, simply because He said it and act upon it. If you can believe God "hath given us all things that pertain unto life and godliness," and get hold of by faith, the exceeding great and precious promises of God," His power will constantly be visible in your life (II Peter 1:3-4).

The world is looking for people who believe God's Word and are willing to take up their positions as ambassadors for Christ and share it with others. We were born into this world for this purpose, for this time. God's glory is being manifested for that very purpose. Colossians 2:3 tells us God has equipped us with his Word which is his wisdom and knowledge, and Colossians 2:10 tells us we are complete in Him. We don't need anything more! God is no respecter of persons, and His presence and power is available to every believer.

The new birth is not a physical or a mental experience. It is a spiritual experience, and in John 3:6 Jesus said, ". . . that which is born of flesh is flesh; and that which is born of spirit is spirit." And after that experience we are required to do something about our minds and our bodies.

In Romans 12:1-2, Paul says:

> I beseech you therefore, brethren, by the mercies of God, that
> you present your bodies a living sacrifice, holy, acceptable
> unto God, which is your reasonable service.
>   And be not conformed to this world: but be ye transformed
> by the renewing of your mind, that you may prove what is
> that good, and acceptable, and perfect will of God.

Just what is the good, and acceptable, and perfect will of God? God's Word is His will, and we are to do what it instructs us to do. Paul is making the point to us that we need to do something with our bodies and our minds. Man's spirit is born again at the New Birth, but he still has the same body and the same soul. You are to present your body to God, and you are to see to it that your mind is renewed with the Word of God. Why, you might ask, would I do something like that?

I Corinthians 6:19-20 (AMP) asks and answers the same question.

> Do you not know that your body is the temple (the very sanctuary) of the Holy Spirit Who lives within you, whom you have received [as a gift] from God? You are not your own.
>
> You were bought with a price [purchased with a preciousness] and paid for, made His own'. So then, honor God and bring glory to Him in your body.

Notice, you are not your own, your body is no longer yours. It belongs to God, which now allows you to erect a "no trespassing" sign on it and tell the devil he has no right to trespass on God's property. Any time he tries to put anything on it just tell him you do not allow anything on it which does not come from God! You present your body to God by requiring it to be dominated by your spirit. You never let your body dictate to your spirit, never let your body tell you what to do. Your physical body did not become born again in the New Birth, so it will want to keep doing the wrong things it is used to doing. Remember, the life of God is in your spirit, so speak to your body and require it to obey the Word of God. You tell it what it can and cannot do, and when you get to the point where your spirit is dominating your body, you will no longer desire to fulfill the lusts (pressures) of the flesh (Galatians 5:17; Romans 12:1-2, 13:12-14).

Notice, in I Corinthians 9:27 Paul said, "I keep under my body, and bring it into subjection." Now, if your body was the real you he would have said, "I keep myself under, I bring myself into subjection." But that is not what he said. He said, "I keep under my body, and bring it into subjection." He brought his body into subjection to his spirit. He didn't let his body dictate to or dominate him; rather, his spirit dictated to and dominated his body.

When God makes the inward man a new creature through the New Birth, the Holy Spirit comes to dwell in that spirit to give it power, which will enable it to dominate the outward man.

You must learn to listen to your spirit and let your inward man dominate your life. And you must make yourself available to go and do what God is asking you to do, and to be willing to be interrupted and be inconvenienced if it means you can minister to or help meet the need of somebody else. I believe this is what Jesus was referring to in Luke 9:23 when He said, "If any man will come after me, let him deny himself, and take up his cross daily, and follow me" (Colossians 3:5-8; I Thessalonians 4:3, 5:22; I Peter 2:11-12).

Galatians 5:16-18 instructs us:

> This I say, walk in the Spirit and you will not fulfill the lusts if the flesh.
>
> For the flesh lusts against the Spirit and the Spirit against the flesh; and these are contrary to one another, so that you do not do the things that you wish.
>
> But if you be led by the Spirit, you are not under the law (Romans 8:2, 8:13-14; Galatians 3:13).

This is important because, "For he who sows to his flesh will of the flesh reap corruption, but he who sows to the Spirit will of the Spirit reap everlasting life (Galatians 6:8 NKJV). You have the choice to either be led by your flesh or by your spirit. It is up to you!

To be led by God's Spirit, you must look beyond what you think, how you feel, and what you want. You must go deeper and discern just what God is saying to you in your spirit. Given, you would like God to agree with what you want. But if God doesn't, you should also be willing to say no to what He is saying no to. God does know just what is best for you and He sees the end from the beginning. He would never lead you into something that you wanted to do just to disappoint you. He is always trying to lead you into the best life you can have.

You renew your mind by meditating on the Word of God. To meditate means to murmur, to ponder, speak, talk, study, utter. You renew your mind by flushing out what the world says about God and the things of God and replacing it with the truth directly from the Word of God. To meditate the Word is to envision yourself having what God's Word says you can have even though you don't see it yet. You have to see it in your spirit before you will receive it (Joshua 1:8; John 17:17).

Many people's minds have never been renewed with the Word of God. They may be saved, filled with the Holy Ghost, and may be members of a good church, but their minds still need to be renewed with the Word of God.

II Corinthians 10:4-5 tells us:

> For the weapons of our warfare are not carnal, but mighty through God to the pulling down of strongholds;
> Casting down imaginations, and every high thing that exalteth itself against the knowledge of God, and bringing into captivity every thought to the obedience of Christ.

Many people are in a battle between their head and their heart. This is spiritual warfare, and these verses say our weapons are not carnal, or natural. They're not guns, swords, or even fists. But our weapons are mighty through God to the pulling down of strongholds. Paul is referring to the "casting down of imaginations." Imaginations can also be translated reasonings, which involve people's minds.

"Casting down every high thing that exalts itself against the knowledge of God" is talking about any kind of knowledge that exalts itself against the knowledge of God and His Word. It's talking about human knowledge here which some people call "sense knowledge." If it is in opposition to what God's Word reveals to you, reject it, cast it down, or throw it away. We are to bring every thought into captivity to the obedience of the Word of God, not just the ones we choose. The goal of every Christian should be to tear down those negative things your soul is using to control your life, and when you do, you will find you have been living with a false sense of security, because the walls of the strongholds were protecting deception and denial in your soul. Don't be surprised to learn Satan has been using them regularly to attack and discourage you. For as long as Satan can hold you in the area of reason, he will defeat you in every battle. But if you hold Satan in the arena of faith, you will defeat him in every battle, and you do that by casting down imaginations (reasoning's).

Are your thoughts and imagination shaped by what you've seen in the movies or on TV or by the negative words of other people? Or, are your thoughts shaped by the Word of God? Romans 12:2 talks about renewing your mind, or changing what you think about so your thoughts are the same as God's thoughts. When your mind is renewed by the Word of God, what you think will be the same as what God thinks (I Corinthians 2:16; Ephesians 4:22-23; Joshua 1:8).

Romans 12:2 "And be not conformed to this world; but be you transformed (changed) by the [entire] renewing of your mind, that you may prove what is that good, and acceptable, and perfect will of God." You can't talk about change without talking about renewing your mind. The renewing of the mind is not a one time event; it is a lifetime process. "For to be carnally minded is death, but to be spiritually minded is life and peace (Romans 8:6).

The Hebrew word translated "*restoreth*" in Psalm 23:3 and the Greek word translated "renewed" in Romans 12:2 have just about the same meaning. For example, a valuable old car or truck which looks like it's ready for the salvage yard can be restored. After the restoration has been completed, it has been renewed. A man's spirit is never restored; it's born again, or recreated. But your soul, which consists of your mind, your will, and your emotions, are restored when your mind becomes renewed with the Word of God. It is vitally important for you to renew your mind, because it is the Word of God that restores souls, renews souls, and saves souls.

> For the word that God speaks is alive and full of power [making it active, operating, energizing, and effective]; it is sharper than any two-edged sword, penetrating to the dividing line of the breath of life (soul) and [the immortal] spirit, and of joints and marrow [of the deepest parts of our nature], exposing and sifting and analyzing and judging the very thoughts and purposes of the heart (Hebrews 4:12 AMP).

Remember, the Word of God has within itself the power to do what it says it will do, but nothing will happen without our participation (Romans 1:16; Hebrews 4:12). When you speak those same words God has spoken, you give them the ability to penetrate down into your soul and do the work God created them to do.

Between Matthew 6:25 and verse 34 you are instructed to "take no thought" of your life, what you shall eat, or what you shall drink; nor for what you will wear or for tomorrow. It all starts with thoughts, and Proverbs 23:7 tells us "For as a man thinketh in his heart, so is he." For out of the abundance of your heart, your heart will produce the results of what you have been feeding it. So what God wants you to do is always think in terms of what His Word says, so that you will always prosper. The failure in your life will always start with a thought in the direction opposite to that of the Word of God. You must build yourself up in the Word of God to the point that when a negative thought enters your mind, your heart will recognize it for what it is and send God's Word out of your mouth to stop that negative thought from taking root in your heart. You are in control of what is on your mind. You have the ability to clean your mind by "sanctifying and cleansing it with the washing of the water by the Word." When your intent is to see things on earth brought into alignment with God's plans in heaven, you will get results every time (Proverbs 4:20-23; Ephesians 5:26).

Note: How you became what you are:

Your thoughts become your words,

Your words become your actions.

Your actions become habits.

Your habits become your character.

Your character becomes your destiny or what you are now.

You take a thought by saying it! Matthew 6:31 tells us, "Take no thought saying." So when you get a stomach ache or your stomach starts to roll don't say something like, I am coming down with the flu or a stomach ache. If your throat started to ache, don't say, I am coming down with a sore throat. If your head started to throb don't say, I am coming down with a headache. No, open your mouth and start confessing what Jesus has already done for you. You say, praise God, your Word says, in I Peter 2:24, "by whose stripes you were healed." This "you" that this verse is talking about is me. I have been healed by the stripes of Jesus and I receive my healing now, according to Mark 11:25, "what thing soever you desire when you pray, believe that you receive them and you shall have them." I receive my healing, and In Jesus' Name, I confess the healing power of God's Word is at work on the inside of me.

In Jesus' Name I take authority of those unseen forces working against me, and I bind them and cast them down, and I declare that no weapon of Satan that is formed against me shall prosper, and nothing shall by any means hurt me, no accident shall overtake me, and nothing shall by any means hurt me, for I have the angels, the ministering spirits, holding me up in their hands least I dash my foot against a stone. Finally I take a few minutes to give God all of the glory and praise for what he has done for me.

Always speak the desired end results!

Use this principle in all areas of your life. Anytime you hear a negative report that is not in line with the Word of God, attack it with a positive confession of faith!

Read the 91st Psalm again. That first verse is talking about you! Are you willing to put and keep God first place in your life?

When you can confess to God, "You are my refuge, You are my fortress, You are my God and in You do I place my (complete) trust," without any doubt you will see Him working in your life every day. The 91st Psalm is loaded with promises from God for you, but you must meet the requirements of the first verse to tap into them. You must dwell (live) in the secret place of the Most High (His Word) and abide (remain stable and fixed) under the shadow of the Almighty. In other words, you must put God in first place in your life and keep Him there!

If you desire to have or possess a thought in your spirit based on the Word of God, your first step is to think about it, and your second step it to say it. You think about it and then you say it, you think about it and then you say it, you think about it and then you say it. You do it over and over until it becomes a habit.

Then you will get to the point when something happens suddenly those words will flow out of your mouth without you even thinking about it, and those words will allow Jesus to intercede for you and interject God directly into the solution to the problem.

7

WHAT IS THE GOD KIND OF LOVE?

Thou shalt love the Lord thy God with all thy heart, and with all thy soul, and with all thy mind (Matthew 22:37).

Thou shalt love your neighbor as yourself (Matthew 22:39).

Love, from the Greek is *agapao*. Any time you see the word love used in a verb form it is from, *agapao,* which means to totally give ourselves over to. Thou shalt totally give yourself over to the Lord thy God—spirit, soul, and body.

It is what we bind ourselves with or become one with.

It is total commitment or consumption.

It is in every sense of the word "fanaticism".

It is what we put first in our lives.

It is a commitment to love. It can be to God or man or things.

It is a word that says I am committed and bind myself to it until we become one. Commitment is love—binding yourself to, tying yourself to—until you become one with; that's how God is asking you to love Him. He is asking you to love Him. He is asking you to bind yourself to Him until you become one with Him. And it is impossible to tie or bind yourself to God until you become one like Him, but we oftentimes choose to tie or bind ourselves to other things.

Let love be without dissimulation. Abhor that which is evil; cleave to that which is good.

> Be kindly affectioned one to another with brotherly love; in honor preferring one another;
>
> Not slothful in business; fervent in spirit; serving the Lord (Romans 12:9-11).

Here is the same verse from the Amplified Bible.

> [Let your] love be sincere (a real thing); hate what is evil [loath all ungodliness, turn in horror from wickedness], but hold fast to that which is good.
>
> Love one another with brotherly affection [as members of one family], giving precedence and showing honor to one another.
>
> Never lag in zeal and in earnest endeavor; be aglow and burning with the Spirit, serving the Lord.

Showing yourself friendly to other people allows God to use all of you. The more of yourself and your life you release to Him, the more you will be fulfilled and experience His peace and joy.

Being "fervent in spirit" is linked to being kind to one another. Kindness is a form of love, and love must be an action. It's not just what you say that matters, it's what you do. When you love and care for the soul of someone you don't even know, you are truly walking in kindness. It is what it means to God that matters most. He is pleased when you show kindness and affection to others.

Brotherly love prefers another over yourself. It is losing sight of yourself for the sake of Christ. You are honoring God's heart's desire, which is to touch the world, and that means when you support those who have answered the call to "go into all the world and preach the gospel to every creature" you are showing your love for all mankind (Mark 16:15). It is about so much more than just money. It's a sign of your love, affection, and brotherly love for the world. True love is helping the helpless and giving to those in need without any thought of getting anything in return; guarding your mouth never to say or repeat anything you do not know to be the truth and showing respect to others the way you want them to treat you.

The place to start is simply asking God every morning to show you how you can be a blessing to somebody else today because love gives without fear or hesitation.

8

THE COST OF LOVE

There is a cost or heavy price paid to tying yourself to God and desiring His will for your life even above your own happiness. God is seeking people who are pure in heart and He has created you to be dependent on Him, to bring to Him your challenges, and allow Him to help you with them. There is a price to pay for a pure heart, but it is well worth it because, "Eye hath not seen, nor ear heard, neither have entered into the heart of man, the things which God hath prepared for them that love him" (I Corinthians 2:9).

The long term results will exceed anything you can conceive, but you have to will yourself to walk in love (Matthew 10:22; Luke 21:17). God has created you to be dependent upon Him, to bring Him your challenges, and allow Him to help you with them. Only He knows what is in your heart, and He is an expert at removing the old junk from your life while retaining what is valuable.

If you have been criticized for believing God and walking in His love, don't let the critics drag you down. That criticism is just the devil trying to bring you back down to your former level. Don't accept their condemnation. If people are talking bad about you, just don't listen, and if they write lies about you, just don't read them, for "there is no condemnation for those who are in Christ Jesus." As long as you are doing right by God, it isn't anybody's business. Accept who and what you are "in Christ" and be confident in the good things that Jesus has done for you (Romans 8:1; John 10:10; Hebrews 13:6).

We know how He gave us the commandment in Matthew 22:37 & 39. He said we are to "love the Lord thy God with all thy heart, and with all thy soul, and with all thy mind. And thou shalt love thy neighbor as thyself."

Did you notice He didn't say anything about your feelings; nor did He say you had to like them. He said that to love is a commandment, not a request. You are to do it whether you like it or not. I John 4:12 tells us, "If we love one another, God dwells [lives] in us and His love is perfected in us."

You may think you have a good reason to violate the commandment of love. It is up to you to either deal with those reasons or to turn your back on God and go your own way. There is no excuse; God's commandment to love your neighbor does not come with any ifs, ands, or buts. God's requirement is for you to say, "yes sir," and do it. You are to love them by command, and when you do, God will begin to expand your inner man, His anointing will begin to work on the inside of you, and you will get to the place in life that you will pay little or no attention to what anybody does or says. The real you is your spirit, and if you will allow your spirit to be led by the Holy Spirit and require your mind and body to act in accordance to the Word of God, the fruit of your spirit will be love, joy, peace, longsuffering, gentleness, goodness, faith, meekness, and temperance.

Notice love is a fruit, it grows and it reproduces itself in your spirit (Galatians 5:22-23). It is when you allow your mind and body to be in control that the works of the flesh will be evident in your life. And to prevent that, "you present your body, a living sacrifice holy acceptable unto God, which is your reasonable service" (Galatians 5:16-21; Romans 12:1; II Corinthians 5:15).

Here is the battle you must win: you must conquer the lust of your flesh and walk daily in the leadership of the Holy Spirit. Galatians 5:16-18 tells us, "Walk in the Spirit, and you shall not fulfill the lust of the flesh. For the flesh lusts against the spirit and the spirit against the flesh; and these are contrary to one another, so that you do not do the things that you wish. But if you are led by the Spirit, you are not under the law."

As a Christian, you must allow yourself to be led by the Holy Spirit that lives in you. If not, then you will revert back to your old status and act like one who has never been born again. Never should you as a Christian allow the old man, your flesh, be the controlling factor in your life. When you give into fleshly human desires and appetites, you are invalidating your new birth.

I Corinthians 5:17 tells us, "Therefore, if any man (person) be in Christ, he is a new creature; old things are passed away; behold all things are become new." The new birth is a supernatural change in the person who has truly accepted Jesus Christ as their Lord and Savior.

Jesus has already won the victory and you must learn how to stand in that victory when the devil comes against you. You must learn how to firmly position yourself in the overcoming power of God. God is your Creator! He is your Savior! He is your Healer and Provider! He is whatever you need, when you need it. The Word of God tells us that God is Love. The more of His Spirit and presence you allow to flow through you, the more you will enjoy and be an expression of His love, joy, peace, longsuffering, kindness, goodness, faithfulness, gentleness, and self-control (I John 4:6-9; Galatians 5:22-23).

By letting His Spirit flow through you, you will become a light in this dark world. Simply refuse to be discouraged by the darkness around you. Set your heart and mind on the Lord, because that is what will bring you peace. Let His Spirit flow through you, and it will help you be a light in this dark world.

Whatever the devil does or says isn't more powerful than the God you serve. Life's problems don't compare and can't compete with God's answers. Remember to exercise passionate faith and declare that you are already delivered! See yourself with what Christ has already done for you and remind yourself that, through Him, you've already won.

9

DEVELOPING YOUR RELATIONSHIP WITH GOD

What kind of relationship do you have with God, with yourself, and ultimately with others?

Keeping your relationship with Jesus alive from day to day is what is going to change your life; otherwise, you're going to struggle through life. You don't need to do that; you don't need to beat yourself in the head and feel guilty for falling down and making mistakes. Jesus is here to be your friend. He has reconciled you and brought you into divine favor with God (II Corinthians 4:16, 5:18), and He is available when you need Him. He said He would never leave you nor forsake you (Hebrews 13:5; Romans 8:38-39).

> Because he has set his love upon Me, therefore will I deliver him; I will set him on high, because he knows and understands My name [has a personal knowledge of My mercy, love, and kindness—trusts and relies on Me, knowing I will never forsake him, no, never].
>
> He shall call upon Me, and I will answer him; I will be with him in trouble, I will deliver him and honor him.
>
> With a long life will I satisfy him and show him My salvation (Psalm 91:14-16 AMP).

Notice the limits that He has placed on this promise? He will never leave you nor let you down. Wow! So, ". . . be strong in the Lord [be empowered through your union with Him]; draw your strength from Him [that strength which His boundless might provides]" (Ephesians 6:10 AMP).

If and when you develop a relationship with Jesus, anytime the devil attacks you with temptation or bombards your mind with wrong thoughts, you will always find Him available; His strength will help you (Philippians 4:13). He can and will do mighty works in you and through you, but you have got to give Him the honor and praise. When you honor and obey the Lord, you are worshiping Him. Romans 12:1 tells us we are to "present our bodies as a living and holy sacrifice, acceptable to God, which is your spiritual service of worship." When you live your life holy unto the Lord by obeying His commands, you are presenting your body to Him and worshiping Him.

Life is about choices, and the Christian life is about putting Christ first place in your life. The more you call on Jesus, and the more you bring the Word of God into your day-to-day life and apply it, the better off your life will be here on the earth. Matthew 6:33 (AMP) tells us "But seek (aim at and strive after) first of all His kingdom and His righteousness (His way of doing and being right), and then all these things taken together will be given you besides." We are being directed to seek first of all the kingdom of God or His ways and His means of doing things; then, His righteousness or your right standing or your rights and privileges as a son of God will be added to you (Romans 14:17; I Corinthians 4:20). Notice that the kingdom of God is a system and the kingdom of Heaven is a place?

Living for God isn't hard, and it has many wonderful benefits. In the natural we make life a lot harder than it really is. Christianity is not about moral ethics. Morality is a by-product because Christianity is a person, not a religion. When you get to the point where you understand what happened to you at the new birth, when your spirit man was reborn into the image and likeness of God, you will live your life a whole lot differently than you do now. If an impulse to sin or a wrong thought popped up in your mind, you would tell yourself "No" and immediately cast it down because you would know that Jesus, the person, is right there in you, and you would want to keep yourself in line with the Word of God. You don't resist because of some "moral code" or "Church doctrine." You resist because you understand the reality of "Christ" living on the inside of you. Before you can resist temptation, you have to know Jesus, the person, and understand or recognize that He is the reason you are saved. He is the reason for your desire to follow or obey the Word of God, for without Jesus, life is meaningless. Christ must be alive in you otherwise there is no hope of you ever experiencing the glory or the manifest presence of God in your life.

I Thessalonians 5:19 tells you to "quench not the spirit" because the Spirit of God lives in your spirit if you are a born again child of God. To quench is from the Greek word *shennumi*, to suppress or subdue, extinguish, put or shut out, to look with contempt upon the gifts and or not allow the gifts to function or be used in the body. It also means to ignore what the Spirit is telling you to do and to go your own way.

I say it again, your body and soul are to be led by your spirit, not the other way around. You are to crucify your flesh and be led by your spirit (Romans 8:13-14; II Corinthians 5:14).

I Peter 5:6 instructs us, "Humble yourselves therefore under the mighty hand of God, that he may exalt you in due time." If you refuse to humble yourself and change your ways to line up with the Word of God, you are a person who does not fear nor reverence God (Psalm 55:19; III John 2). To "humble yourself" is from the Greek, *tapeinooo,* which means to demote, or lower yourself in your own estimation.

Is God first in your life? In your F-finances, I-interests, R-relationships, S-schedule, T-troubles? If you can say that God is first in these five areas of your life, then it is a pretty good sign that God is first in all your life! If not, you need to get into the Word of God and find out which areas need some binding and loosing.

10

GOD'S LOVE DEMANDS DISCIPLINE

For the Lord corrects and disciplines everyone whom He loves, and He punishes, even scourges, every son whom He accepts and welcomes to his heart and cherishes.

You must submit to and endure [correction] for discipline; God is dealing with you as with sons. For what son is there whom his father does not [thus] train and correct and discipline?

Now if you are exempt from correction and left without discipline in which all [of God's children] share, then you are illegitimate offspring and not true sons [at all]" (Hebrews 12:6-8 AMP). [Proverbs 3:11-12.]

When God disciplines you, it is proof He loves you. It is proof that you are His son or daughter. If God has never disciplined you it is because you are not His, you are not spiritual. You don't even know God. Remember you will never get so mature in Christ that He will no longer correct you when you need it.

God uses His word to discipline us. Read II Corinthians 7 as an example.

II Timothy 3:16 (AMP) tells us,

Every scripture is God-breathed (given by His inspiration) and profitable for instruction, for reproof and conviction of sin, for correction of error and discipline in obedience, [and] for training in righteousness (in holy living, in conformity to God's will in thought, purpose, and action).

He uses the Spirit power in His Word to correct you in ways to make you strong, not weak and condemned. So yield yourself to the Word of God and let it correct you and remove the fleshly lusts that can lead you astray.

If you want to experience God's best for your life, you must learn to pay attention to the warnings God placed in your heart. On the inside of you there is an alarm system, and anytime you get into an area of compromise, or other questionable areas, that alarm will go off down in your spirit, and you will feel an uneasiness, which is God speaking to you. He is trying to let you know you are approaching some sort of danger and that you need to make some sort of an adjustment in your life.

A lot of the problems that may come up in your life can be avoided if you will discipline yourself; if you will listen to and heed the warnings God is giving you—which will often require a minor adjustment in the direction of your life before it is too late.

I encourage you to be a person of integrity and take the high road and don't settle for second best. Wherever you go and whatever you do, God is always right there with you (Colossians 2:20).

The problem might be as simple as watching a TV show or movie of questionable moral value, driving over the speed limit, not being completely honest in your dealings with others, or thinking about things you shouldn't. It is the little things in life which add up to be the big problems. You have got to submit your will to God's will and obey Him in order to hear His voice clearly and see His will done in your life. For "Happy and fortunate is the man whom God reproves; so do not despise or reject the correction of the Almighty [subjecting you to trial and suffering]" (Job 5:17-27 AMP).

Learn to notice when God is disciplining you. He is doing it to help you. He loves you and corrects you in love, and He will keep you from evil if you will put your trust in Him.

Again, when you do mess up, and you will, don't run and hide but run to God. He has his arms stretched out to you (I John 1:9). God's mercy is just and real. If you will let Him, He will always forgive you and cast the memory of any wrong doing out of His mind (Isaiah 43:25; Jeremiah 31:34).

When you knowingly disobey God's instructions, you step out of His will, and you are saying, "I want what I want more than I want what God wants for me and I know what is best for me." But you don't know what is best for you; you will find that the green grass across the road is often times deceptive. Being led around by your flesh, instead of what the Spirit of God is saying often makes for an unhappy life.

Make the decision: "If it isn't from God, it isn't for me." God will never steer you wrong. Your job is to "Trust in the Lord with all thine heart; and lean not on thy own understanding. In all thy ways acknowledge him, and he shall direct thy paths." So, stick it out when you feel like quitting, and finish your course with joy, "for the joy of the Lord is your strength" (Nehemiah 8:10; Proverbs 3:5-8).

Start confessing: "I am strong in the Lord and the power of His might and I can do all things through Christ which strengthens me. For God is at work in me, creating in me the power and the desire, both to will and to work for His good pleasure" (Ephesians 6:10; Philippians 4:13, 2:13).

God has provided you with spiritual armor which will allow you to "be strong in the Lord, and the power of His might." But, it is your choice to use it or let it set. You must choose to clothe yourself with God's armor, God's Word, and know and be confident that every time the devil comes against you, you will always come out on top. God loves you that much! (Ephesians 6:10-18).

Did you notice the above verses do not say anything about you being physically strong? Don't allow yourself to slip back into the natural and try and do it yourself. If you try to hold on or stand against the devil in your own strength, you will get worn out after a while and suffer defeat. Allow yourself to bask in God's strength, be strong in the Lord and the power of his might, and watch the devil go down in a ball of flames (Ephesians 6:10).

"Bodily exercise profits a little, but godliness [walking in love] is profitable for all things, having promise of the life that now is and of that which is to come (I Timothy 4:8 NKJV). Bodily exercise profits us only in this life, while godliness or walking in love is profitable not only in this life but also when we get to heaven.

Living for God means keeping His Word. If we are going to live for God, we've got to keep His commandments. Under the Old Covenant they had the 10 Commandments, but under the New Covenant the only commandment we are required to keep is the law of love! But to keep the commandment to love God and to love our neighbor we must use the 10 commandments as a guideline.

11

What is love

As you read I Corinthians 13: 4-8 from the King James Edition and the Amplified Bible. Replace the word "charity or love" with "<u>The God kind of love that the Holy Spirit has injected into me</u>".

4. "Charity suffereth long, and is kind; charity envieth not; charity vaunteth not itself, is not puffed up,

AMP. Love endures long and is patient and kind; love never is envious nor boils over with jealousy; is not boastful or vainglorious, does not display itself haughtily.

5. Doth not behave itself unseemly, seeketh not her own, is not easily provoked, thinketh no evil;

AMP. It is not conceited—arrogant and inflated with pride; it is not rude (unmannerly), and does not act unbecomingly. Love [God's love in us] does not insist on its own rights or its own way, for it is not self-seeking; it is not touchy or fretful or resentful; it takes no account of the evil done to it—pays no attention to a suffered wrong.

6. Rejoiceth not in iniquity, but rejoiceth in the truth;

AMP. It does not rejoice at injustice and unrighteousness, but rejoices when right and truth prevail.

7. Beareth all things, believeth all things, hopeth all things, endureth all things.

AMP. Loves bears up under anything and everything that comes, is ever ready to believe the best of every person, its hopes are fadeless under all circumstances and it endures everything [without weakening].

8. Charity never faileth:"
AMP. "Love never fails—never fades out or becomes obsolete or comes to an end."

From the Message Bible, Check yourself out, how do you measure up?

"Love never gives up." How easy do I give up?
"Love cares more for others than for self." Am I selfish or self centered?
"Love doesn't want what it doesn't have.**"** Am I content with what I have?
"Love doesn't strut." Do I act like I am really something special?
"Doesn't have a swelled head." What do I think about myself?
"Doesn't force itself on others." Am I pushy?
"Isn't always "me first." Am I selfish and self centered?
"Doesn't fly off the handle." How well do I control myself?
"Doesn't keep score of the sins of others." Do I have a list?
"Doesn't revel when others grovel" What is my attitude?
"Takes pleasure in the flowering of truth" Am I always honest?
"Puts up with anything." What is my limit?
"Trusts God always." Is God in first place in my life?
"Always looks for the best (In others)." How do I perceive others?
"Never looks back" Am I willing to forget the past?
"But keeps going to the end." Am I determined to run the race to the end?

Check other translations of the Bible and reread and meditate these verses again and again and think about how God expects you to act and how He sees you through the eyes of His love for you. You can actually see God's nature in these verses, here God is telling us to be more like He is. And by obeying His Word to love Him and to love your neighbor as yourself you will become more like He is, because you have the nature of God in you.

Did you notice that the degree of how much you love is based on your actions? Love is not just a feeling—it is a set of behaviors and choices. You must will to love someone; it does not just come automatically. Remember, the Holy Spirit is in you to help you if you will follow His leading.

The world's definition and the Bible's definition of love are two entirely different things. The world's definition of love has to do with your feelings, and this human love often stops when we get into a situation where we are not comfortable. The human kind of love is quite selfish or conditional; it is based on comfort or how one makes us feel. The Bible's definition of love is based on your actions.

The God kind of love is not based on how you feel, but on the fact you are to love God, love yourself, and love everybody else. But first you must know God loves you, and you must receive the love that God has for you. Make up your mind right now to receive this injection, the love of God, from the Holy Spirit, and allow it to expand and grow in your life.

God knows we can't give away something we don't have, so He chose to love us first. The simple statement—Jesus loves me—is so remarkably hard for us to believe. A lot of people, deep down inside, really don't like themselves, and they cannot comprehend that God loves them just as they are. Love is expressed in many different ways, but one factor is always the same; love gives (John 3:16).

1 John 4:10 says, "Herein is love, not that we loved God, but that he loved us, and sent his Son to be the propitiation (the sacrifice) for our sins." People of the world are looking for something real and tangible. These people are looking for love, and God is love. God's love is so real that even in the hard times, we are comforted by the knowledge God loves us and we no longer have to live in fear. In other words, the cycle of love begins with God. His love for us is what ignites within us a love for Him and a love for others. Receiving His love is what enables us to obey Matthew 22:36-40.

So, how much does God love us? John 17:23 tells us He loves us just as much as He loves Jesus. Verse 23, ". . . and hast loved them, as thou hast loved me."

If you take the time to meditate I Corinthians 13:4-7 and get a good grasp of what love really is, then John 17:23 should literally knock your socks off when you realized how God looks at and feels about you (John 3:16).

Take an inventory of your thoughts and beliefs; think about how you feel, and think about God's attitude toward you, and compare it with what His Word says.

John 17:26 says, "And I have declared unto them thy name, and will declare it: that the love wherewith thou has loved me may be in them, and I in them." Jesus is saying here that He is praying for them and everybody who will come to Him through their words (Romans 10:9-10); that He is going to the cross and will be raised from the dead for this purpose; "that the love that You, God the father, has loved me, Jesus Christ, may be in them and I in them." The love He has for His perfect Son is in each one of us, and we have been authorized to use it with which to love others.

John 17:20 tells us Jesus was not only praying for the 12 apostles but for all who would believe in Him. So confess this, "Jesus has qualified me to contain the very love with which God loves Jesus with and He lives in me." (Say it over and over.)

When you look at yourself in this perspective, you will realize God is not looking at you the same way you look at yourself.

II Corinthians 4:6-18 tells us we have this treasure in earthen vessels, the God who commanded the light to shine out of darkness, has commanded the light to shine in us. (Author's translation).

You need to keep your eyes on the prize of heaven and trust God to prepare you so God's glory will be revealed through your life. God loves you just the way you are, and no matter what happens in your life, if you are obedient to walk in God's will, you can trust everything will work out because of His great love for you. Remember,

> He is a shield to all those who take refuge and put their trust in Him (Psalm 18:30).

And we are directed to,

> Trust in the Lord with thine heart; and lean not unto thine own understanding.
> In all thy ways acknowledge him, and he shall direct thy paths.
> Be not wise in thine own eyes: fear the Lord, and depart from evil.
> It shall be health to thy navel, and marrow to thy bones (Proverbs 3:5-8).

"Thine [or your] own understanding" is your reasoning, your thinking, or the thoughts that cross through you head or mind. This verse is directing you to trust in the Lord with your heart (your spirit) and not what is in our head!

II Corinthians 10:5 instructs us, as part of our spiritual warfare to "... cast down [these] imaginations [reasoning's], and every high thing that exalteth itself against the knowledge of God, and bring into captivity every thought to the obedience of Christ." Paul is referring to "casting down imaginations." Imaginations can also be translated as *reasonings*, which involve your minds. Simply put, we are to bring our thoughts into captivity to the obedience of the Word of God. If you have a thought that does not line up with the Word of God, you reject it!

The devil can and will beat you every time if he can keep you in the arena of reason. But if you hold him in the arena of faith, you will defeat him in every battle. And you do that by casting down those imaginations, by keeping the Word of God first place in your mind and in your mouth.

12

RECEIVING GOD'S LOVE

To receive the love of God, start right now by looking at yourself in a mirror and saying aloud, "God loves me, I am loved by God and God loves me as much as He loves Jesus!" Just keep saying it over and over and thanking God for it until the truth of it begins to saturate your heart and then it will start building a confidence in your heart and in your life. That confidence will rise up in you, come out of your mouth, and come out in your actions. We are in this life together with God. John 17:23 says, "I in them, and thou in Me." That is the Father, His son the Lord Jesus Christ, the Holy Spirit you and me. And when you do, I can almost guarantee you that the devil will come around and try to steal the Word out of your heart. Mark 4:15 tells us ". . . but when they have heard, Satan cometh immediately, and taketh away the word that was sown in their hearts." Don't give his lies any place in your thinking (II Corinthians 10:5). Stop the devil in his tracks by saying aloud,

> I praise the Holy Name of Jesus, for "Greater is he that is in me than he that is in the world." Greater is the great God almighty, creator of the heavens and the earth and all that is within. Greater than all the demons and demonic spirits who know nothing but to kill, steal, and destroy.
>
> Father, I praise You and I thank You for loving me so much. I thank You, Lord, for giving Your own Son, Jesus, that I might not perish but have everlasting life. I receive Your love for me right now, in Jesus' Name.

Don't ever let the devil deceive you into thinking God or Jesus loves someone else more than they do you. Jesus has never violated the commandment to love everybody equally, and He requires it from us also. Jesus loves you because His Father commanded Him to do it before the foundation of the world. He loves His Father and He loves you as he loves His own self.

John 15:10 says, "If you keep my commandments, you shall abide in my love, even as I have kept my Father's commandments, and abide in His love." The bottom line is you have to keep God's commandments and abide in His love and believe God's love abides in you. He wants to be your first love. He wants you to love Him with all your heart, with all your soul, and with your entire being. Believe the love that God has for Jesus actually abides in you, and the creative principle of the heavens, the very love of God Himself, has been imparted into your spirit, and you have been authorized to love others with it. And when you start receiving and believing God's love, you will experience His presence and His love. When you know God loves you, you won't find it hard to have a personal relationship with Him. And then you will find it isn't a struggle to return his love and to love Him in kind. God wants you to depend entirely on Him; God wants you to lean on, trust in, and rely on Him. When God says you can do nothing apart from Him, He means things will not work properly in your life unless you invite Him into your everyday life and commune with Him in daily fellowship. Never be afraid to say, Lord, I can't do this without you.

Take the time to abide in his presence. Look for shorter and more direct ways of doing things which will allow you more time to fellowship with God, and make use of all the tasks in your daily life to show Him that love, and allow His presence to be in you by the communion of your heart with His. Keep your life simple. God is very interested in helping you deal with your weaknesses.

We are instructed in Hebrews 3:12-14 (AMP):

> [Therefore, beware] brethren, take care, least there be in any one of you a wicked, unbelieving heart [which refuses to cleave to, trust in, and rely on Him], leading you to turn away and desert or stand aloof from the living God.
>
> But, instead warn (admonish, urge, and encourage) one another every day, as long as it is called today, that none of you may be hardened [into settled rebellion] by the deceitfulness of sin [by the fraudulence, the stratagem, the trickery which the delusive glamour of his sin may play on him].

> For we have become fellows with Christ (the Messiah) and share in all He has for us, if only we hold our first newborn confidence and original assured expectation [in virtue of which we are believers] firm and unshaken to the end.

You will have to remind yourself over and over in your thoughts and with your words that God loves you. When you change your thoughts and your words you will change your life! And as you gain a greater revelation of God's unconditional love for you, you will see a breakthrough in your relationship with those around you, and you will let your guard down and allow God's love to flow through you to others. God's love is far too amazing and to good too be held as a private possession. Remember, to love is not a feeling, it's your choice.

I Corinthians 6:19 tells us "that your body is the temple of the Holy Ghost which is in you," and Paul wrote in Romans 5:5 "the love of God is shed abroad in our hearts by the Holy Ghost which is given unto us." Something may be permissible but at the same time it may not be helpful or profitable for us. But if we walk in wisdom and in God's love we will not live in regret.

> Whosoever shall confess that Jesus is the Son of God, God dwelleth in him, and he in God. And we have known and believed the love that God hath to us, God is love; and he that dwelleth in love dwelleth in God and God in him (I John 4:15-16; John 17:23; Romans 10:9-10).

Consider these verses concerning God's love for you. Read them and consider just what God has done for and given to you. You are somebody when you are "born again" and it takes Jesus to make something out of you and you must allow the Holy Spirit to direct you into the direction that Almighty God wants you to go. That His love for you is so great, even in hard times it is a comfort to know God loves you and you do not have to walk in fear. You must get yourself so saturated in the 'God kind of love" that you will:

> . . . let all bitterness, and wrath, and anger, and clamor and evil speaking, be put away from you, with all malice: And

be ye kind one to another, tenderhearted, forgiving one another, even as God for Christ's sake hath forgiven you. Be ye therefore followers of God, as dear children; and walk in love, as Christ also hath loved us, and hath given himself for us an offering and a sacrifice to God for a sweet smelling savour (Ephesians 4:31-5:2).

RULES FOR LIVING A HOLY LIFE

Also take the time to read Colossians 3 from the Amplified Bible.

1. "If you then be risen with Christ, seek those things which are above, where Christ sitteth on the right hand of God" (Ephesians 1:20).

Ephesians 2:6 (AMP) says, God "hath raised us up together with Him and made us sit down together [giving us joint seating with Him] in the heavenly sphere [by virtue of our being] in Christ Jesus (the Messiah, the Anointed One)."

If you let the Word of God live in your heart and mind, it will give you insight to intelligence and wisdom. It will help you keep a good attitude. If you want a good life then you must keep your mind on good things, God's Word.

2. "Set your affection on things above, not on things on the earth."

Confess: As for me, I choose to have God's best for my life. I choose to walk in the light of life (John 8:12).

How is your life? Is it different now that you are a Christian? God has changed you from your old life into a new creation. Ask God to help you put off the old you and put on the new you which was created in His image.

3. "For you are dead, and your life is hid with Christ in God."

Because you are "in Christ" and Christ is in you, you are dead to sin and alive to righteousness. Spiritually speaking you are now dead to sin but alive unto God through Jesus Christ (Romans 6:2 and 11; II Corinthians 4:10).

4. "When Christ, who is our life, shall appear, then shall you also appear with him in glory" (John 14:6).

Who shall? What a great promise! You must be determined to be victorious and refuse to settle for anything less than the best God has for you.

You must be active. Start thinking the right thoughts and set your mind on the things of God.

5. "Mortify therefore your members which are upon the earth; fornication, uncleanness, inordinate affection, evil concupiscence, and covetousness, which is idolatry" (Romans 6:13, 8:13; Ephesians 5:3 and 5).

You do this by yielding these areas of your life to Christ and confessing God's Word and confessing Jesus as Lord over these areas of your life.

6. "For which things sake the wrath of God cometh on the children of disobedience" (Ephesians 2:2; I Corinthians 6:11).

7. In the which you also walked some time, when you lived in them.

8. But now you also put off all these; anger, wrath, malice, blasphemy, filthy communication out of your mouth" (Numbers 4:28; I Thessalonians 5:22; Ephesians 4:22 and 29).

God has given each one of us specific responsibilities. What specific responsibilities has God given you in the various areas of your life? Ask Him to help reveal these to you and to fulfill those various areas of your life which are not pleasing to Him. Many people do not understand we are three-part beings, spirit, soul, and body. We are a spirit, we have a soul (composed of our mind, will, and emotions) and we live in a body. God wants your spirit to be filled with His Spirit and your spirit to be in control of your soul and body.

9. "Lie not one to another, seeing that you have put off the old man with his deeds" (Ephesians 4:22 and 29; Proverbs 6:17).

Think about your life before you became a Christian. How different is your life now? You must be determined to have victory and refuse to settle for anything less than the best of what God has for you. If you want the good life, then you must keep your mind on good things. Many believers want the good life, but many people just set around wishing for something good to happen. You must be active not passive (Matthew 6:33).

10. "And have put on the new man, which is renewed in knowledge after the image of him that created him" (II Corinthians 5:17; Romans 12:2; Ephesians 2:10; 4:23).

Notice, you put on the new man. You change the way you act, you change the way you think. You determine the direction your life will take for the rest of your life here on earth. God will not force you to do anything. If you really want to know what direction your life is going, just listen to the words you speak.

11. "Where there is neither Greek nor Jew, circumcision nor uncircumcision, Barbarian, Scythian, bond nor free: but Christ is all, and in all" (Acts 10:34; Ephesians 1:22-23; Galatians 3:28).

God is no respecter of persons, with Him the playing field is level.

12. (You) "Put on therefore, as the elect of God, holy and beloved, bowels of mercies, kindness, humbleness of mind, meekness, longsuffering" (I Peter 1:2).

13. "Forbearing one another, and forgiving one another, if any man have a quarrel against any; even as Christ forgave you, so also do you."

God will only forgive you with the same measure you use in forgiving others! God will only be as quick or slow to forgive you as you are in forgiving those who have sinned against you (Luke 11:4).

14. "And above all these things put on charity, [Love] which is the bond of perfectness." The Amplified Bible says, ". . . which binds everything together completely in ideal harmony" (I Peter 4:8; I Corinthians 13:13; Ephesians 4:3).

15. "And let the peace of God rule in your hearts, to the which also you are called in one body; and be ye thankful" (Ephesians 4:4, 4:7; I Corinthians 7:15; I Thessalonians 5:18).

16. "Let the word of Christ dwell in you richly in all wisdom; teaching and admonishing one another in psalms and hymns and spiritual songs, singing with grace in your hearts to the Lord" (Ephesians 5:9).

17. "And whatsoever you do in word or deed, do all in the name of the Lord Jesus, giving thanks to God and the Father by him" (I Corinthians 10:31).

Every Christian is born into the body of Christ by the blood covenant of Calvary. We are blood brothers and sisters and it is impossible to be separated by race, wealth, or position because we are one "in Christ." Jesus prayed in

John 17:21, "Father that the church may be one as You and I are one that the world may know that You have sent me." Remember, God loves that other person just as much as He loves you.

18. "Wives, submit yourselves unto your own husbands, as it is fit in the Lord" (Ephesians 5:3; I Peter 3:1).

Marriage is covenant agreement between two parties and the marriage covenant is the most important covenant you will make on this earth. A covenant woman fears the Lord. Proverbs 31:31 says "A woman who fears the Lord is to be praised." She is strong both spiritually and morally.

19. "Husbands, love your wives, and be not bitter against them" (Ephesians 4:31, 5:25).

A covenant man loves his wife just as Christ loved the church and gave Himself for it. If you do not love your wife, then you are in rebellion against God. Self love destroys God's love. A covenant man will put his wife's and children's best interests ahead of himself. He will gladly give his life for their betterment.

In marriage, both the man and woman have to crucify their own will for the relationship to be strong. God will bless covenant fathers and mothers for having the spiritual strength to shape the destiny of their children.

20. "Children, obey your parents in all things: for this is well pleasing unto the Lord" (Exodus 20:12; Ephesians 6:1-2; Proverbs 21:3).

This is the only commandment that comes with a blessing.

21. "Fathers, provoke not your children to anger, least they be discouraged" (Ephesians 6:4).

The most challenging and rewarding relationship can be with your family members. Ephesians helps us deal with our families in a Godly way.

22. "Servants, obey in all things your masters according to the flesh; not with eye service, as according to the flesh; but in singleness of heart, fearing God" (Ephesians 6:5; Titus 2:9, 3:1; I Timothy 6:1; I Peter 2:18).

This includes your boss or supervisor at work. You need to be real, sincere, honest, and trustworthy at all times.

23. "And whatsoever you do, do it heartily, as to the Lord, and not unto men. Be prepared for and willing to do any upright and honorable work" (Ephesians 6:6-7).

24. "Knowing that of the Lord you shall receive the reward of the inheritance: for you serve the Lord Christ" (Ephesians 6:8; I Corinthians 7:22).

25. "But he that doeth wrong shall receive for the wrong which he hath done: and there is no respect of persons."

Notice again, it is your choice of action which generates the required reactions.

(Romans 2:11; Ephesians 6:9; I Peter 1:17; Deuteronomy 10:17).

Verses 18, 19, 23, 24 show us a Christian renders service to others as a way of serving the Lord, Jesus Christ. In these verses, the relationship to which this truth is specifically applied is to the husband-wife relationship. The role and admonition God assigns to a husband is meant to be a way of serving the wife. Likewise a distinctive role and direction is given to the wife, according to which she serves her husband. These roles are not self-chosen; nor are they assigned by the culture in which one lives: they are given by God as a means of manifesting the life of Christ on the Earth. In this setting, the word "submission" acquires its full biblical significance for family life. Husband and wife alike are submissive to God in fulfilling the roles He has given them. In serving one another, husband and wife serve and honor Christ. The word "submit," from the Greek *hupotasso* is formed from *hupo* (under) and *tasso* which means, "to arrange in an orderly manner". In this context, it describes a person who accepts his or her place under God's arranged order. Submission is not limited to wives only. In James 4:7 and Ephesians 5:21, we see the directive applied to every believer, in their relationships with others and in their relationship with God (I Peter 3:1-7; Hosea 2:16-20).

> The person who has My commands and keeps them is the one who [really] loves Me; and whoever [really] loves Me will be loved by My Father, and I [too] will love him and will show (reveal, manifest) Myself to him. [I will let Myself be clearly seen by him and make Myself real to him] (John 14:21 AMP).

13

HOW ACTING OR NOT ACTING IN LOVE AFFECTS YOUR LIFE

You will find, as you look back upon your life, that the moments when you have really lived are the moments when you have done things in the spirit of love.

Henry Drummond.

The Ten Commandments are the Law of God for all generations without exception. They hold the secret to our world's survival! They are not God's recommendations; they are God's commandments. To reject them is to reject Him and to reject Him is to guarantee our moral destruction.

The whole of the Bible is reduced to 10 proclamations from God to man. Historically, civilizations which have obeyed these 10 proclamations have prospered and flourished, while civilizations which disobeyed these 10 proclamations have been crushed and buried in the bone yard of human history!

"Blessed is the nation whose God is the Lord (Psalm 33:12).

[Read: Deuteronomy 28 to see a more complete picture].

The Ten Commandments hold the secret to a sweeping moral and spiritual awakening in America, but the Body of Christ needs to step up, practice them and teach them to others. Matthew 5:19 teaches us, ". . . he who practices them and teaches others to do so shall be called great in the kingdom of heaven." To do otherwise is very dangerous (Romans 1:22).

In Egypt, Pharaoh owned the Hebrews, they were His property. As such, are you in Egypt right now? Are you a slave to sin? Are you controlled by the sin in your life?

"No servant can serve two masters; for either he will hate the one and love the other, or else he will be loyal to the one and despise the other. You cannot serve God and mammon" (Luke 16:13). The question is, whose servant are you, Jesus Christ's or Satan's? There is no middle ground!

Moses came as a deliverer to the children of Israel. The same way Jesus Christ came to deliver us when He Demanded that Satan release us from the bondage of sin at the Cross of Calvary.

Moses demanded that Pharaoh release the children of Israel from the bondage of Egypt and once the children of Israel were delivered from Egypt, they passed through the Red Sea. After experiencing salvation from Egypt by walking through the Red Sea, which was a type of water baptism, they departed from Egypt and its bondage. God did not take the Hebrews out of Egypt to do their own thing; He took them out of Egypt straight into Sinai in order to attach them to the 10 Commandments and the Torah. Similarly, God does not offer us salvation through His Son so we can become masters of our own universe. Nobody is ever free until they are mastered by something greater than themselves! As such, you are never free until you are bound to God and Christ by the command to love God and love your neighbor as yourself which encompasses the Ten Commandments.

I ask you again, are you a servant of Jesus Christ or of Satan himself? Are you a slave to the sin in your life and addictions? Or is your life a reflection of God's grace and mercy?

> I call heaven and earth to record this day against you, that
> I have set before you life and death, blessing and cursing:
> therefore choose life that both thou and thy seed may live
> (Deuteronomy 30:19).

Notice here God has given you the choice. It is your decision to choose life or death, blessings or cursing. Proverbs 18:21 tells us "Death and life are in the power of the tongue: and they that love it shall eat the fruit thereof." Your words have power! (Romans 10:9-10; I John 4:15; Matthew 10:32, 12:37).

Nobody can make these choices for you and you will learn you have to make these choices almost every day. It is the little problems in your life which accumulate to become the big problems. God has given us ten simple rules to eliminate the little problems in our lives. If obeyed, they will give us a much richer life here on earth. In the Song of Solomon 2:15 these little problems are referred to as "the little foxes that spoil the vines."

What this mean is that people are typically not destroyed by what they would consider big issues in life, but by a series of smaller seemingly insignificant choices or compromises which build up to become those big issues. Watch for those little foxes in your life! Little foxes can ruin a strong, healthy vine.

As you read the 10 Commandments, remember, God has set before you life and death, so choose life (Deuteronomy 30:19).

1. "I am the Lord your God, Who has brought you out of the land of Egypt, out of the house of bondage. You shall have no other gods before or beside Me.

2. You shall not make yourself any graven image [to worship it], or any likeness of anything that is in the heavens above, or that is in the earth beneath, or that is in the water under the earth; You shall not bow down yourself to them or serve them; for I the Lord your God am a jealous God, visiting the iniquity of the fathers upon the children to the third and fourth generation of those who hate Me, But showing mercy and steadfast love to a thousand generations of those who love Me to keep My commandments.

3. You shall not use or repeat the name of the Lord your God in vain [that is, lightly or frivolously, in false affirmations or profanely]; for the Lord will not hold him guiltless who takes His name in vain."

Do you want to see the power of God released when you speak His name? The name of the Lord represents awesome power, and we need to reverently fear it. Ask God to reveal to you the power and weight of His name. When you do use it, honor it and remember how awesome it is.

4. [Earnestly] remember the Sabbath day, to keep it holy [withdrawn from common employment and dedicated to God].

Six days you shall labor and do all your work,

But the seventh day is a Sabbath to the Lord your God; in it you shall not do any work, you, or your son, your daughter, your manservant, your maidservant, your domestic animals, or the sojourner within your gates.

For in the six days the Lord made the heavens and earth, the sea, and all that is in them, and rested the seventh day. That is why the Lord blessed the Sabbath day and hallowed it [set it apart for His purposes].

5. Regard (treat with honor, due obedience and courtesy) your father and mother that your days may be long in the land the Lord your God gives you.

6. You shall not commit murder.

7. You shall not commit adultery.

8. You shall not steal.

9. You shall not witness falsely against your neighbor.

10. You shall not covet your neighbor's house, your neighbor's wife, or his manservant, or his maidservant, or his ox, or his donkey, or anything that is your neighbor's (Exodus 20:2-17 AMP).

The Ten Commandments are encapsulated in the commandment to love God and love our neighbor as we do ourselves and they are positive principles, they are the blueprint to your success, and God is directing you in these things for a reason. It is only when you receive the revelation of how your life is affected and how it works will you know how to use it to your benefit. It is when you obey these commands that you demonstrate your love for God.

Take a few minutes to judge yourself using these commandments as a guideline. We are reminded in I Corinthians 11:3, "For if we would judge ourselves, we would not be judged" (Luke 6:37).

The New Covenant includes all but one of the Ten Commandments—the fourth one, which concerns the Sabbath Law. This commandment was left out of the New Testament because it was strictly a sign between God and Israel. The ceremonial law of the Sabbath described in Exodus 31:13-18 was subsequently fulfilled in Christ. The Sabbath was the time God made as a covenant reminder that God would restore back to man through Jesus Christ the completeness of Him resting in God's provision. Now we are living in that Sabbath and we are or should be in the rest of God. Jesus taught us the laws of the Kingdom of God and now we are to operate in those laws to our benefit (Hebrews 4:1-11).

The early Christians set aside the first day of the week to assemble for worship (Acts 20:6-12; I Corinthians 16:1-2). We observe the Sabbath on the first day of the week, because it was on the first day of the week that Jesus arose from the grave and gained victory over death, hell, and Satan. It is on that day that we entered into our rest in Christ; and God desires that we continually abide in His rest—not just on Sunday, but everyday of the week (Colossians 2:14-17; Hebrews 4:1-11).

The commandment to love God deals with the first four of the Ten Commandments; and the commandment to love your neighbor as yourself deals with the next five; and the tenth commandment deals with your thoughts.

The conclusion of every matter is to love the Lord with all of your heart, with all your soul, and with all your mind, and to love your neighbor as yourself.

Ecclesiastes 12:13 tells us, "Fear God, and keep his commandments: for this is the whole duty of man." To "fear God" is to have a reverential respect for Him. Your reverential respect for God is your foundation for happiness. When you respect somebody you will have a tendency to listen to what he or she has to say and use those words as a guide to your actions. "The fear of the Lord is the beginning of wisdom: a good understanding have all they that do His commandments: his praise endureth forever" (Psalm 111:10; Job 28:28; Proverbs 1:7; Matthew 22:37-38; Revelations 14:7). There are many benefits from the characteristics of the fear of God. One, who fears God, has a built-in restraint against yielding to anything evil. In other words, one thinks twice before doing or saying something they know to be wrong. The fear of God works well with Holy Spirit conviction. Reverential respect of God and Holy Spirit conviction helps one stay out of trouble and aware of God's divine order for their life.

> The Fear of the Lord prolongs days, but the years of the wicked shall be shortened (Proverbs 8:13, 9:10, 10:27).

> The Fear of the Lord is a fountain of life, to depart from the snares of death (Proverbs 14:27).

> Better is little with the fear of the Lord than great treasure
> and trouble there with (Proverbs 15:16).

The fear of God is a characteristic that should be natural to mankind, both saint and sinner. It's your choice!

Examples: In the Garden of Eden, Eve allowed Satan's cunning lie to override her fear of God and Adam's natural love for Eve overrode his fear of God; and just look at the trouble their lack of fear has brought upon mankind.

Noah and his family evidently feared God and obeyed Him. Noah, without fear could have reasoned himself out of the assignment to build an ark; after all it had never rained. Noah feared God and was obedient.

Maintaining a healthy respect and reverence for God produces many wonderful results! Numerous things may reflect a loss of the Fear of God. One's thoughts and actions of carnality, materialism, worldly pleasures, and lust indicate the fear of God is diminished. Consider the immorality now in our churches and you will quickly realize there is no fear of God there.

After a lifetime of trying things the world has to offer, Kathy and I have come to the realization that no one can find any lasting enjoyment apart from God. The best way to spend your life is to fear God; to listen to and obeying Him. Your highest purpose and your most noble duty is to turn your back on the world and spend your days in the reverential fear of God and by obeying Him. I encourage you to make this the number one priority in your life. (Psalm 19:9, 111:10; Proverbs 1:7, 9:10, 10:27, 14:26, 15:16 & 33, 19:23, 22:4).

The Redneck version of the Ten Commandments:
1. There ain't but one God.
2. Put nothing before God.
3. Watch your mouth.
4. Get yourself to the Sunday meetin'.
5. Honor your Ma and your Pa.
6. No mudderin'.
7. No fooling around with someone else's lady or feller.
8. Don't take what ain't yours.
9. No telling of tales or gossipin'.
10. Don't be hankerin' for other people's stuff.
[Author unknown.]

14

The Blessings or the Curses

Read all of Deuteronomy 28. To make my point I am only going to print out verses 1, 2 and 15. It is very important for you to read and study the rest of this chapter and get to know and recognize the blessings of obeying God's commands and the curses which will come upon your life and those of your descendants after you if you choose not to obey. Also read the 2nd commandment in the previous chapter.

Ephesians 2:10 tells us we "are God's workmanship, created in Christ Jesus unto good works, which God hath before ordained that we should walk in them". What are those good works? Those good works are found in Deuteronomy 28:1-2 &14. That is a picture of how God intended for us to live upon this earth!

1. <u>If you will listen</u> diligently to the voice of the Lord your God, <u>being watchful to do</u> all His commandments which I command you this day, the Lord your God will set you high above all the nations of the earth.

2. <u>And all these blessings shall come on thee</u>, and overtake thee <u>if thou shalt</u> <u>harken</u> unto the voice of the Lord thy God.

15. But it shall come to pass, <u>if thou wilt not harken</u> unto the voice of the Lord thy God, <u>to observe to do</u> all His commandments and His statutes which I command you this day, that all these curses shall come upon thee and overtake thee.

Notice the words "if you will listen" and "being watchfully to do." This requires action on your behalf. You are making the decision to be "set high above all above all the nations of the earth," or to receive "all these curses that shall come upon thee and overtake thee." This should go a long way's in explaining why things happened to many people. To harken is to listen to and act upon!

Remember, in the first chapter where in Matthew 16:19, we are to allow only those things into our lives that God allows in Heaven. You choose to allow a blessing or a curse into your life by the choices you make. In Ephesians 1:3, we see ". . . God the Father of our Lord Jesus Christ has blessed us with all spiritual blessings in heavenly places in Christ." As you read Ephesians 1:3, did you notice God has already blessed us? Past tense; it's already done! Those blessings are yours but you have to allow them to come upon you by speaking God's Word over your life and doing what God has purposed for you to do until the manifestation comes. The blessing will work things out if you don't give up. It is up to you to walk in the result of those blessings.

Being *blessed* is to be empowered to prosper as a result of having God's favor bestowed upon your life. A blessing is an empowerment and carries the idea of permanent happiness, whereas a curse is also an empowerment and carries the idea of permanent sorrow and pain.

Proverbs 26:2 (NAS) says, "So a curse without cause does not alight" or a curse doesn't just happen. There is a reason behind it. A curse is a blessing blocker which will only occur when there is a cause. When Jesus died on the cross, He paid the price and provided you with a better covenant, which doesn't carry a curse any more. Galatians 3:13 tells us, "Christ hath redeemed us from the curse of the law." Now read verses 16 thru 68 from Deuteronomy 28, and see what Jesus has freed you from. They include every diabolical thing the devil could ever use to destroy you. These are the things God has healed you of and delivered you from. But you must receive them into your life by faith and walk in the benefits of them. Jesus paid the price for them when He bore the curse. He became the blood covenant sacrifice for you by proving once and for all just how much He loves you and desires to bless you. Just receive it and let Him bless you exceeding and abundantly above all you can ask or think.

The bottom line is: Love is the mainstream of the blessings of God in which He will manifest Himself to you. God wants you blessed! And those blessings won't come upon you without your authorization, and you authorize it by obeying God's instructions. If you want the blessings of God to come on you and overtake you, then you must be willing to meet the conditions. If you are not willing to harken, observe, or to do what God says, then He is under no obligation to bless you or empower you to prosper. Remember, God has set the rules, and the rules were not set by God to be a hardship on you. God has set the rules because once you meet them, once the conditions are met, the pressure is off you and on the devil. Once you have met the conditions God has set, you will receive the guaranteed results. Notice, now that you have met the conditions who has the pressure on them? Not you! The pressure is on the devil. And there is nothing he can do to stop the results if you have met God's conditions.

There are requirements to be met before you receive the promises of God, but they are not there to make it hard on you. They are there to make it hard on the devil. God's promises usually come with conditions and He is merciful and just, and He does certain things for us that we do not deserve (Psalm 118). So harken diligently, observe, and do. If you will do these things, then the blessings will come on you and overtake you. It's only a matter of time. He gives you the ability to do the things He calls you to do. Your part is simply to listen to His voice and do what He says without reservation. That's when the blessing comes.

Now God wouldn't ask you to do it if you couldn't, because you can do it! You can meet the requirements for receiving God's blessings by doing it God's way. Notice in Philippians 4:13 (AMP), "I have strength for all things in Christ Who empowers me [I am ready for anything and equal to anything through Him Who infuses inner strength into me; I am self-sufficient in Christ's sufficiency]." God will never ask you to do something that He will not provide you with all of the support you require. That is His grace and mercy in action!

If you decide to try this, you are setting yourself up for failure. To try something indicates there is a time limit involved in which you have no intention of carrying it through to completion.

Living the Christian life is a lifestyle which never ends!

15

THE REWARDS OF OBEDIENCE

You shall love the Lord your God with all your heart, and
with all your soul, and with all your mind.

This is the first and great commandment.

And the second is like it: You shall love your neighbor as
yourself (Matthew 22:37-39 NKJV).

It was Jesus Himself who taught us to love and not hate. In Matthew
19:19, He instructs us to . . . "love your neighbor as yourself," and in John
15:12 He instructs us to, "love one another as I have loved you," and in verse
14 He tells us "Ye are my friends, if you do whatsoever I command you."

One of the problems many people have today is that they do not think
well of themselves. We need to know God's word teaches us to love ourselves.
If you do not like yourself, you will have a hard time liking anyone else.
You may pretend you do, but sooner or later the truth will come out. We
must keep the right attitude toward others and also the right attitude toward
ourselves. We are simply free to be the person God has created us to be. We
are also free to love ourselves, which enables us to love others.

Jesus was even more direct in Matthew 5:4-5, where He instructed: "But
I say to you, love your enemies, bless those who curse you, do good to those
who hate you, and pray for those who spitefully use you and persecute you,
that you may be sons of your Father in heaven."

Hatred is simply not an option for people who want to serve God and
have His blessings upon their lives. When we read the commandment of love
as a new believer, you must admit that you know very little about it. But
as you began to meditate on it, confess it, and align your life with it, that
command will begin to root itself in your mind and heart. And if you will

stick with it, eventually you will become so grounded in the commandment of love that you will judge your whole life by it. And when that happens, if someone says something ugly to you, for example, instead of lashing out at them, you will start searching for a way to keep the commandment and respond to them in love. When you do, God's love will be perfected in you (I Thessalonians 5:15; I John 4:12).

When someone doesn't treat you right, you have a golden opportunity to help heal a wounded heart. Keep in mind: People who are in pain often hurt other people. If someone is rude or inconsiderate, you can almost be certain that they have some unresolved issues inside. The last thing they need is for you to respond angrily.

Some people are like garbage trucks; they run around full of garbage, anger, frustration, and disappointment. As their garbage piles up, they need a place to dump it, and sometimes they'll dump it on you. Don't take it personally. Just smile, wave, wish them well, and move on. Never make the mistake of taking their garbage and spending the day spreading it around to your family and friends.

The more you practice yielding to love, the stronger your revelation of God's love grows. Your comprehension of it increases, and as a result your life is increasingly filled with the fullness of God and you will come out far ahead of where you would have been had you tried to fight fire with fire.

You will notice successful people do not let garbage trucks take over and control their day. They realize life is too short to wake up in the morning with regrets, so they choose to love the people who treat them right and forgive the ones who don't.

Don't just read through the following verses; but read them aloud to yourself over and over, meditate on what they are telling you, and make your decision to love God and your fellow man based on what they are saying to you.

> But I say unto you which hear, Love your enemies, and do good to them which hate you.
> Bless them that curse you, and pray for them which despitefully use you (Luke 6:27:28).

> And as ye would that men should do to you, do you also to them likewise (Luke 6: 31).

In Luke 6:27 we are taught how to deal with our enemies. Something is missing when we say we forgive those who have hurt or offended us and go no further, even though God tells us in His Word to forgive others. He goes on to instruct us to bless them. In this context the word "bless" means to speak well of. One of our problems is that, though we pray and try to forgive those who offend us, we turn right around and curse them with our tongue or rehash the offense again and again with others—which is gossip. Remember, anyone who will gossip with you will gossip about you!

To work through the process of forgiveness, and enjoy the peace we seek, we must do what God tells us to do: not only to forgive but also to bless those who hurt and mistreat us. One reason we find it so hard to pray for them is we tend to think we are asking God to bless them physically or materially. The truth is we are not praying for them to make more money or gain more possessions; we are praying for them to be blessed spiritually. What we are doing is asking God to bring truth and revelation to them about their attitude and behavior—thereby enabling them to repent and be freed from their sins. When we forgive and pray for them, we bless not only them, but ourselves also.

Note: We will deal with how to pray for these people in the last chapter of the book.

> See that none render evil for evil unto any man; but ever follow that which is good, both among yourselves, and to all men (I Thessalonians 5:15).

> Be not deceived: God is not mocked: for whatsoever a man soweth, that shall he also reap (Galatians 6:7).

If you sow love, you will reap love. If you sow hate and discontent, you will reap hate and discontent. II Corinthians 9:6-8 is both a warning and a wonderful promise. God is a God of abundance, not lack. Ask Him to give you a cheerful heart as you give and increase your faith to see abundance for every good work.

> He which soweth sparingly shall reap also spairingly; and he which soweth bountifully shall reap also bountifully.

Every man according as he purposeth in his heart, so let him give; not grudgingly, or of necessity: for God loveth a cheerful giver.

And God is able to make all grace abound toward you; that you, always having all sufficiency in all things, may abound to every good work (II Corinthians 9:6-8).

Knowing that whatsoever good thing any man doeth, the same shall he receive of the Lord, whether he be bond or free (Ephesians 6:8).

But he that doeth wrong shall receive for the wrong which he hath done: and there is no respect of persons (Colossians 3:25).

Therefore judge nothing before the time, until the Lord come who will bring to light the hidden things of darkness, and will make manifest the counsels of the hearts: and then shall every man have praise of God (Mark 4:22).

Let every soul be subject unto the higher powers. For there is no power but of God: the powers that be are ordained of God (I Corinthians 4:5).

Whosoever therefore resisteth the power, resisteth the ordinance of God: and they that resist shall receive to themselves damnation (Romans 13:1-2).

Beloved, never avenge yourselves, but leave the way open for [God's] wrath; for it is written, Vengeance is Mine, I will repay, says the Lord (Romans 12:19; Deuteronomy 32:35 I Thessalonians 4:6).

I challenge you to be a maker and maintainer of peace today and every day of your life. God is your avenger; let Him fight your battles. Turn your hurt and pain over to Him, and let Him handle them in His own way. He has promised that He will help you if you put your trust in Him. He will bring justice in your life. And you will be able to abide in God's rest.

. . . seeing it is a righteous thing with God to repay with distress and affliction those who distress and afflict you (I Thessalonians 1:6).

But if anyone has the world's goods and sees his brother and fellow believer in need, yet closes his heart of compassion against him, how can the love of God live and remain in him? (I John 3:17 AMP).

First John 3:16-18 teaches us some things about love. How do you define love? One aspect of love is helping meet the needs of others. It is important to tell people God loves them and you love them; it is also necessary to demonstrate that love through action and good deeds, especially toward fellow believers.

Always be courteous to your fellow man and be honorable at all time, always doing what is right no matter what the cost to yourself.

"If you love me, keep my commandments." (John 14:15.) To whatever degree you love God, to that same degree you will obey Him. To whatever degree you obey Him, that is the measure of your love for Him. As your love for Jesus grows, so will your obedience.

What will happen when you allow God's Word to be in first place and the final authority in your life? I John 2:5 says "But whoso keepeth his word, in him verily is the love of God perfected; hereby know we that we are in him." The love of God will be perfected in your life, and that perfect love will cast out all fear. That is how you will ultimately know that you are in Him, in Christ. "For in Him dwelleth all the fullness of the Godhead bodily and you are now complete in Him which is the head of all principality and power" (Colossians 2:9).

God is directing us to not only love our enemy and bless those who curse us but to forgive them and pray for them and not hold anything against them. It is sometimes hard to forgive some people who have done us wrong, and it is oftentimes hard to release all bitterness and start loving people who have hurt us. But we need to do it anyway. Why? You might ask. It is for the sake of the anointing, the power of God which resides within us (I John 2:27). We need that anointing intact. We need it to guide us and protect us in these dangerous days. Without it, we will fall prey to the devil's devices. And with it, "we will be more than conquerors through Him who loves us." We will be able to shake off every strategy [carefully worked out plan of action] of the devil. We will live in victory.

Forgiveness is often times more for the one doing the forgiving than the one being forgiven. You may have had circumstances in your life where someone has done you a great wrong, and you have a right to be angry and bitter. You may feel as though your whole life has been stolen away from you by someone. But if you will choose to let go of your grudge and forgive him or her, you can overcome that evil with good. You can get to the point where you can look at the person who has hurt you and return good for evil. And if you do that, God will pour out His favor in your life in a fresh way. He will honor you; He will reward you, and He'll make those wrongs right. But if someone does something that offends you, hurts your feelings or does something that you don't agree with, and if you don't cut it off right there, if you don't release the law of love, if you don't keep the commandment to love your neighbor right there, then all of that curse from Deuteronomy 28:15 on, which includes every sickness and every disease, all poverty and all bad things, suddenly has regained some authority in your life, and Jesus is standing there on the side lines almost helpless to do anything about it. And it shall come to pass by your authorization. It is legal now.

It's no longer saying, well, Satan can't make it come to pass, because when you don't respond the way Jesus tells you to respond then you have opened the door and accepted and authorized a curse which someone has spoken over your life and given it power and authority.

This very commandment is an act of the love of God saying, I don't want you cursed I want you blessed. So when someone releases a curse your way, the way for you to cut it off is to authorize a blessing to come forth on him or her.

What he is trying to do is to sow a seed in your life, and if you join him by retaliating, you are watering his seed. You are allowing that seed, that curse, to take root, grow, and to blossom in your life, and allow the root of bitterness to come up. If you don't break that thing off it will eat your life up.

You might ask, how do we let this happened? It is actually a very simple process. So simple, in fact, you might wonder why we seem to have such a difficult time with it. Why, you might think, do we so quickly and so often lose sight of this all important commandment of love?

The devil gets involved, that's why. He is always working to sabotage your love walk. John 10:10 tells us he comes only to kill, steal, and destroy.

To get a better understanding of how he does it, read the parable of the sower from Mark 4:14-20.

> 14. "The sower soweth the word.
>
> 15. And these are they by the way side, where the word is sown; but when they have heard, <u>Satan cometh immediately</u>, and taketh away the word that was sown in their hearts.
>
> 16. And these are they likewise which are sown on stony ground; who when they have heard the word, immediately receive it with gladness;
>
> 17. And have no root in themselves, and so endure but for a time: afterward, <u>when affliction or persecution</u> ariseth for the word's sake, immediately <u>they are offended</u>.
>
> 18. And these are they which are sown among thrones; such as hear the word.
>
> 19. And <u>the</u> <u>cares of this world,</u> and <u>the deceitfulness of riches</u> and the <u>lusts of other things</u> enter in, choke the word, and it becometh unfruitful.
>
> 20. And these are they which are sown on good ground; such as hear the word, and receive it, and bring forth fruit, some thirty fold, some sixty, and some an hundred.

The stony ground in verse 16 refers to a heart that is easily offended; and is often referred to as people who "wear their feelings on their shirtsleeves." Nothing fruitful will be able to grow and produce a good life in this type of environment. But you can avoid this trap of offense, you can recognize this plan of the devil to rob your harvest and keep you from receiving God's promises.

You determine what type of soil your heart is by how willing you are to believe and act on what the Word of God says. How willing are you to open your heart to God and do what He is asking you to do? How willing are you to overcome the afflictions and persecution the devil is going to throw at you?

It takes no more energy to believe God can and will do something for you than it does to believe He can't or won't. So why not use your energy on exerting your faith, which will help you overcome, instead of spending it on doubt and unbelief, which will only end in defeat. When you become impatient, frustrated, and fretful, it will be because you are trying to make something take place that only God can make happen (Isaiah 40:31).

Unbelief, which is fueled by fear and doubt, will ruin your future if you allow it to happen! In its simplest form, unbelief is simply fear. And you have to stop allowing fear to convince you God's promises aren't real and that God won't come through for you.

Your goal should be to know, understand, and operate in the power and authority Jesus reclaimed for you at Calvary. Jesus said in John 14:12-14, "The things that I do, you shall do also." Understand, if it were not possible, Jesus would not have said it.

Mark 4:15-19 reveals the devil's method of operation. It show us that as soon as the seed of God's Word is planted in your heart, he starts working to get rid of it. He starts trying to dig it up before it has a chance to take root.

Did you notice what tool the devil uses to achieve this? The tools of affliction and persecution (II Timothy 3:12; Mark 10:29)! Affliction and persecution are nothing more than the devil trying to get your mind off of the Word of God. They are an expression of Satan's terrible fear of all born-again Christians (Mark 4:19; Matthew 5:11; Ephesians 6:12; James 2:19).

He sends a person along to offend you by saying something mean to you which will hurt your feelings, or he gets someone to irritate and provoke you until you step over into strife. Surprisingly it is often a family member or a close friend.

The word "devil" in the Greek carries the idea of a constant irritation, poking, pressing or pecking away at something in order to penetrate and get entrance into it. And the word "offense" is defined as "the name of the part of a trap to which the bait is attached, hence, the trap or snare itself." We don't think of offense as being bait or the center of the trap, but once you allow offense to attach itself to your heart, it will stop the power of God from flowing into your life. This is why we all need to continually protect the spiritual condition of our hearts (Psalm 119:11).

This is the way Satan functions. He cannot change his pattern. He goes after the seed of the Word in your heart by poking at you through someone's unkind words or actions. He harasses you with the thoughtless or irritating behavior of others. He pecks at you any way he can. He tries to provoke you into reacting so you'll violate the commandment of love, because when you do, he gains entrance into your life. It enables him to pierce your soul like a thorn would pierce your finger. Then he keeps on working from that place to infect you more and more with his poison.

Ephesians 4:27 tells us, "Neither give place to the devil."

You can choose to not give him a place in your life. You must never lose sight of this in your life, because what you lose, he gains. The Word tells us to resist the devil—it doesn't say we should assist the devil (James 4:7)!

You assist him by giving him time to work in your thought-life. From there, he can gain hold of you and secure a place in your physical doings in life. Understand, you don't have to do that. You can refuse to give the devil a place in your life. If your mind is not filled with God's thoughts and desires it is left empty for the enemy to enter and gain a foothold in your life.

Many times when we have things happened to us we think are unjust, unfair, or unkind, it appeals to the side of us that wants to know why and the majority of the time when we don't get the answer we want, it leads to frustration which often leads to the destruction of our walk and fellowship with God.

We are not to base our walk with God on explanations but by the promises of God because in the majority of situations the explanation won't make any sense to us or help us. Your goal should be to always trust God and not seek answers to all of your problems. You do this by spending quality time with God every day.

> Trust in the Lord with all your heart, and lean not on your own understanding:
>
> In all your ways acknowledge Him, and He shall direct your paths (Psalm 3:5).

Being anxious about your problems will cause you to lose your joy and the devil is looking for those he may devour (I Peter 5:8).

If you want to really hurt the devil, just don't do what he is asking you to do, or do just the opposite. Kick the devil out of your territory and refuse defeat. Enforce the Word of God in your life and refuse to back off until you have what belongs to you. Although the devil may try to discourage you and plant doubt in your heart about God's promises, you can make a quality decision to guard your heart and mouth and refuse to speak defeat. Make it a habit to always speak the promises of God concerning your situation (Colossians 2:6-7).

Remember, the devil is here only, ". . . to steal, and to kill, and to destroy," and he uses "the cares of this world, the deceitfulness of riches and lusts of other things" to distract you (John 10:10; Mark 4:19).

The cares of this world can best be described as your everyday problems and concerns.

The deceitfulness of riches: Riches are deceitful in that many people feel, if they were rich, they would have no problems. When you have no money and you are looking forward to the day when you will have more than enough money, you think you will have no worries or problems. In fact, it is just the opposite. You will still have problems and worries, but they will be entirely different. You will experience a comfort level of not having to worry about your bills every month, but it changes the way people look at and deal with you. When people express interest in you, you will not be able to eliminate or factor out the possibility that it might be your lifestyle or the fact that you have money which is a attracting them. You will always be on the outlook for those people who are trying to separate you from your money. Having money will never separate you from the reality of life and death, because money is nothing but a rate of exchange. You work and receive money in exchange for it, you buy food and clothing, etc, and you exchange money for it. It is not the money you have or do not have that is a problem; it is when you put money up on a pedestal and worship it that it becomes a problem in your life. It is the love of money that is the root of all evil (I Timothy 6:10).

"The lusts of other things:" Lusts are pressures, the pressures of everyday life and the desire to have what you do not have.

As you study the following verses you will see it is God's will for you to seek His kingdom and allow Him to show Himself strong as you do so.

> Seek (aim at and strive after) first of all His kingdom and His righteousness (His way of doing and being right), and then all these things taken together will be given you besides (Matthew 6:33 AMP).

> For the eyes of the Lord run to and fro throughout the whole earth, to show himself strong in the behalf of them whose heart is perfect toward him (II Chronicles 16:9).

God wants to show Himself strong on your behalf when you walk with Him and show that you are fully committed to His Word and His ways. It is God's purpose and great pleasure to shower His great love upon you, but you must receive it by faith, and walk in the light of it today.

Other people are not your problem!

> For we wrestle not against flesh and blood, but against principalities, against powers, against the rulers of the darkness of the world, against spiritual wickedness in high places (Ephesians 6:12).

This verse gives insight into the spiritual war all believers are in. Our enemies are not natural but spiritual. We can never win our battles if we fight against the wrong source in a wrong way. We tend to think people or circumstances are our problem, but the source of many of our troubles is Satan and his demon spirits. We cannot fight him with carnal (natural) weapons, but only with the supernatural ones God has given us for the destruction of Satan's strongholds. Our battle is not just with our emotions, but with the spiritual forces which play on our emotions. This means we war against strong spiritual entities; ". . . the weapons of our warfare are not carnal, but mighty through God to the pulling down of strong holds" (II Corinthians 10:4). To fight this battle we need to put on our spiritual armor as described in Ephesians 6:13-18 and yield ourselves to the power and presence of the Holy Spirit within us as we pray.

Strong holds are nothing but lies we have chosen to believe. And in Matthew chapter 4 verses 4, 7, and 11 Jesus has given us a very good example of how to handle the devil. "It is written."

To win the battle you only need to find the verses in the Bible which pertain to your problem and the victory you have "in Christ" and simply tell the devil, "It is written" and quote the Word to him. Be diligent to study God's word, so you too will know what action to take in order to resist and overpower the devil.

A really good verse to start with is found in Isaiah 54:17.

> No weapon [of Satan] that is formed against thee (me) shall prosper; and every tongue that shall rise against thee (me) in judgment thou (I) shalt condemn. This is the heritage of the servants of the Lord and their righteousness is of me, saith the Lord.

"This is the heritage." Your heritage is your inheritance, your birthright. Galatians 4:7 says you are "a son; and if a son they are an heir of God through Christ." You have been made the righteousness of God in Christ Jesus and you have a right as an heir to all the blessings and benefits which have been provided to you through Christ Jesus.

So stop blaming yourself and feeling guilty, unworthy, and unloved. Instead begin to praise God and say,

> If God is for me who can be against me? God loves me, and I love myself. I am more than a conqueror—I am strong in the Lord and in the power of His might, and I can do all things through Christ who strengthens me. Christ lives in me and I am complete in Him which is the head of all principality and power. I Praise You Lord for I am free in Jesus' name.

Remember, you have been made the righteousness of God in Christ Jesus, and it is up to you to stand on your rights and privileges which have been bought for you by the blood of Jesus. The free gift of righteousness came upon all men through Jesus, but only those who take that gift and act upon it can walk in the benefit of it. Part of your inheritance is to have and enjoy favor. God desires to restore you to favor with Himself so you can act as His ambassador on the earth. You need to look upon yourself as an emissary from a foreign land. The Bible says we were strangers and foreigners here, but now we are fellow citizens with the saints, and are of the household of God. God wants to restore us to favor with Him so we can act as His ambassadors on the earth. The Bible tells us not only are we ambassadors for Christ, but we are Kings and Priests unto our God. This is why we need a different attitude toward ourselves and others because we are God's representatives here on the earth (Ephesians 2:19; II Corinthians 5:20 AMP; Revelation 1:6).

> Behold, I give unto you power to tread on serpents and scorpions, and over all the power of the enemy, and nothing shall by any means hurt you (Luke 10:19).

Serpents and scorpions are nothing but demons and evil spirits. The Amplified version says:

> I have given you authority and power to trample upon serpents and scorpions, and (physical and mental strength

and ability) over all the power that the enemy [possesses],
and nothing shall in any way harm you.

As noted earlier, the word power derives from the Greek *exousia*, meaning authority. The authority on earth that is invested in the Name of Jesus Christ and was obtained by Him through His overcoming Satan at the cross was then delegated by Jesus Christ to the Church. In Matthew 28:18-19, "And Jesus came and spake unto them, saying, all power [authority] is given unto me in heaven and in earth. Go you therefore," as My ambassadors here on the earth. Jesus spoke these words after His death on the cross, after His burial, after His defeat of Satan in hell, after His resurrection, after His ascension with His own blood to the heavenly Holy of Holies, but just before His ascension to be seated at the right hand of the Father. Jesus said that all authority in Heaven and on earth is given to Him. Then He immediately transferred this authority on earth to His Church, saying, "Go ye therefore."

And if you initiate the action and apply the authority and power Jesus has given to you against the demonic spirits and over all the power the enemy possesses, then and only then will "nothing shall by any means hurt you" (Luke 10:19).

God doesn't cause sickness and harm to come upon us. He has given us the authority—the power—to stop it and we, the church of Jesus Christ, as a whole have failed to do our part. Hebrews 2:7-8 tells us God set Jesus over all the works of His hands, and in Matthew 28:18-19, Jesus gave that power and authority to the church, the body of Christ (Hosea 4:6).

God Himself is the power, the force, behind this authority. The believer who is fully conscious of divine authority can therefore face the enemy without fear or hesitation (John 5:19-30). Jesus was always obedient to the Father. The world will take notice if we, as the church of Jesus Christ, His body on the earth, will wage war against selfishness, walk in love, and do what we see the Father doing. Selfishness is the direct opposite of walking in love! The two most powerful forces on the face of the earth are love and selfishness! Learn to recognize selfishness in yourself, for it has the power within itself to stop your spiritual growth. Love activates the law of the Spirit of life in Christ Jesus, while selfishness activates the law of sin and death (Romans 8:20).

Behind the authority possessed by the believer is a power far greater than the power that backs our enemies. And those enemies are compelled to recognize that authority! II Corinthians 5:20 says we "are ambassadors for Christ." Do you know you are Christ's ambassador here on the earth? Just as you were reconciled to God through Jesus, He now entrusts you to tell others that they too, can be reconciled to God and have a personal relationship with Him. You are an ambassador of Christ if you have made Jesus Christ the Lord of your life and you have been sent to be a representative for Him into the world. Just as this country sends ambassadors to represent their interests in other countries you have been sent to look after the interests of the Kingdom of God. Everywhere you go, you represent the Kingdom of God. God has equipped you with His name and the power of His Word. He has put His spirit in you, and He has given you the ability to hear and obey the directions of the Holy Spirit.

If you will give your all to God, He will give you back such an anointing and such power and such glory and such goodness that you will shine for him. Philippians 2:15 says, "That you may be blameless and harmless, the sons of God, without rebuke, in the midst of a crooked and perverse nation, among whom you shine as lights in the world." God says you will shine as lights; and you will be dominated by spiritual glow.

Ask God to show you how to be his representative in everything you do and everywhere you go. You are one of God's ambassadors here on the earth. Jesus has given you all power, and it is your responsibility to carry out His will here on the earth, as it is in Heaven (Matthew 6:10). As an ambassador, you are to obey God and do what He directs you to do, when He wants you to do it, and do it the way He wants you to do it!

Spend time meditating these verses until they are anchored in your soul, and then put them into action by dousing yourself inside and out with the one substance the devil can't stand—the love of God. If you will keep yourself in the love of God, the Bible says the wicked one won't be able to touch you.

> We know [absolutely] that anyone born of God does not [deliberately and knowingly] practice committing sin, but the One Who was begotten of God carefully watches over and protects him [Christ's divine presence within him preserves him against the evil], and the wicked one does not lay hold (get a grip) on him or touch [him]
> (I John 5:18 AMP).

Love will cause the devil to flee. In prayer and in life, love is our mightiest weapon and our greatest defense against the forces of evil. This is what God means in James 4:7 when He says, "Submit yourselves therefore to God. Resist [To stand firm against a person or influence] the devil and he will flee [as if in terror] from you." All human beings have evil tendencies, but James teaches us that God will give us more and more grace to deal with these tendencies.

For the weapon to work properly, however, it's not enough for us just to love the Lord and people who treat us kindly. God calls us to love everyone—even those who intentionally hurt us. Jesus Said:

> You have heard that it was said, You shall love your neighbor and hate your enemy;
>
> But I tell you, love your enemies and pray for those who persecute you.
>
> To show that you are the children of your father Who is in heaven; for life makes His sun rise on the wicked and on the good, and makes the rain fall upon the upright and the wrongdoers [alike].
>
> For if you love those who live you, what reward can you have? Do not even the tax collectors do that?
>
> And if you greet only your brethren, what more than others are you doing? Do not even the Gentiles (the heathen) do that?
>
> You, therefore, must be perfect [growing into complete maturity of godliness in mind and character, having reached the proper height of virtue and integrity], as your heavenly Father if perfect (Matthew 5:43-48 AMP).

Love! Walking in love is walking in God, who is the light of man, who is the Word of God. Keeping the commandment of love, for walking in love and faith is the key to walking in the light of life (I John 1:5; John 1:1-4; 8:12). God is light. So let the light of God shine on your hidden motives and dark places. He knows about them anyway and wants to bring you to a place of freedom.

> He that saith he is in the light, and hateth his brother, is in darkness even until now.
>
> He that loveth his brother abideth in the light, and there is none occasion of stumbling in him.

> But he that hateth his brother is in darkness, and walketh
> in darkness, and knoweth not whither he goeth, because that
> darkness hath blinded his eyes (I John 2:9-11).

Love is the theme of 1 John, but there are things as a believer we are not to love, things that distract you from God and His purpose for your life. Ask God to deepen your understanding and your love for Him and the things of His kingdom

> We know that we have passed over out of death into life by
> the fact that we love the brethren (our fellow Christians).
> He who does not love abides (remains, is held and kept
> continually) in [spiritual] death.
> Anyone who hates (abominates, detests) his brother
> [in Christ] is [at heart] a murderer, and you know that no
> murderer has eternal life abiding (preserving) within him (I
> John 3:14-15 AMP).

> The way we know we've been transferred from death to life
> is that we love our brothers and sisters. Anyone who doesn't
> love is a good as dead.
> Anyone who hates a brother or sister is a murderer, and
> you know very well that eternal life and murder don't go
> together (I John 3:14-15 The Message Bible).

16

OPERATING IN LOVE

Therefore my dear ones, as you have always obeyed [my suggestions], so now, not only [with the enthusiasm you would show] in my presence but much more because I am absent, work out (cultivate, carry out to the goal, and fully complete) your own salvation with reverence and awe and trembling (self-distrust, with serious caution, tenderness of conscience, watchfulness against temptation, timidly shrinking from whatever might offend God and discredit the name of Christ)."

[Not in your own strength] for it is God Who is all the while effectually at work in you, [energizing and creating in you the power and desire], both to will and to work for His good pleasure and satisfaction and delight.

Do all things without grumbling and faultfinding and complaining [against God] and questioning and doubting [among yourselves], That you may show yourselves to be blameless and guileless, innocent and uncontaminated, children of God without blemish (faultless, unrebukable) in the midst of a crooked and wicked generation [spiritually perverted and perverse], among whom you are seen as bright lights (stars or beacons shinning out clearly) in the [dark] world.

Holding out [to it] and offering [to all men] the Word of Life, so that in the day of Christ I may have something of which exultantly or to rejoice and glory in that I did

not run my race in vain or spend my labor to no purpose
(Philippians 2:12-16 AMP).

Just as stars shine brightly against the dark of night, so our lives as Christians should also shine like light in the spiritual darkness of the world. Ask God to help you shine brightly with His love and joy to those around you.

For it is God which worketh in you both to will and to do
of his good pleasure (Philippians 2:13).

He who is in you is working on the inside of you to bring these things to pass. But you have to authorize those dealings which are being worked out in you so it will stop whatever Satan or whatever curses somebody is trying to work against you. So the act of operating in love is for your own protection and benefit from the things you have been redeemed and delivered from coming back on you. Without the gift of salvation, you were destined for eternity in Hell's fire. Although salvation is a free gift, from a loving heavenly Father, it is of more value than all of the wealth in the world. Salvation is the most wonderful and precious gift you can ever possess, and you should never, never take your salvation lightly.

Philippians 2:12 directs us to ". . . Work out your own salvation." Salvation here meaning, "material and temporal deliverance from danger and apprehension, preservation, pardon, restoration, healing, wholeness and soundness."

You have been redeemed, you have been saved—saved from the fiery pits of hell and everything that you need to be saved from. Jesus has redeemed you from the curse of the law (Galatians 3:13), but all of these things are not just going to fall into your lap! They all require action on your part. They require you to build up and exercise your faith in God and your faith in His Word (Jude 20).

Before you can enjoy any real victory over sin and experience change in your behavior, you must learn that only God can change you. You must let God be God in your life.

Confess: "God is working in me as I put my trust in Him, and I believe I am getting stronger every day. God is strengthening me in my weaknesses and helping me overcome bad habits."

Jesus' work at Calvary was a complete work; every problem you could even conceive was covered by Jesus' shed blood on the cross (Isaiah 53:1-6). But all of these things are not just going to fall on you. You are going to have to literally work out your own salvation, which will require action on your part. You have to enforce "the law of the Spirit of life," enforce the devil's defeat, and incorporate what belongs to you. For it is those who are "willing and obedient that eat the good of the land" (Romans 8:2; Isaiah 1:19).

It is seed time and harvest; you are either going to plant a love seed and allow it to grow in your life, or you are going to plant a curse seed and let it grow in your life—and one of the products of that curse seed is fear.

There is a battle going on for your heart, a battle between God and Satan, between good and evil, to see who's word will be the dominating force in your ground, or in your heart. The question is? Will you allow God's Word or the world's word to be the dominating force which will rule your life.

Your life is the sum total of the Word you have allowed to get in through what you have heard, what you have seen, what you have spoken, and what you have allowed to grow in your life. Life is the result of seed planted! This is why God tells you to "keep your heart with all diligence; for out of it are the issues of life" (Proverbs 4:23).

Life itself flows out of man's heart. God once told me, "I have put in your heart My love, [the God kind of love] and I want you to let it flow out of your heart so that it will protect you from being entangled with all the other stuff that is trying to flow into your heart."

There is a battle. Satan knows he can't produce anything in a life unless he can get seed planted into the ground of your heart. If he can get you to be offended, if he can get you into strife, or be angry because of this or that; and if you allow that seed to be planted firmly into your heart, and keep it there until you act on it based on the law of receiving, then Satan will have won. It is what is in your heart that will overcome and overwhelm your life, leaving you wondering, why aren't my prayers answered? Why am I not getting healed and so on?

You must guard your heart aggressively and let your thoughts be only good thoughts—thoughts about things which are honorable and true. Then confess what God says about you and then will your heart attitude will change (Philippians 4:8).

Love is the key to answered prayer. The Bible tells us "We receive from Him whatever we ask, because we [watchfully] obey His orders [observe His suggestions and injunctions, follow His plan for us] and [habitually] practice what is pleasing to Him" (I John 3:22 AMP). When you pray, believe God hears you! This is a promise from God.

> Beloved, if our heart condemn us not, then have we confidence toward God.
>
> And whatsoever we ask, we receive of him, because we keep his commandments, and do those things that are pleasing in his sight.
>
> And this is his commandment, that we should believe on the name of his Son Jesus Christ (The anointed one), and love one another, as he gave us commandment.
>
> And he that keepeth his commandments dwelleth in him, and he in him. And hereby we know that he abideth in us by His Spirit which he had given us (I John 3:21-24).

This is speaking to us about condemnation in our heart. A condemned heart steals confidence. You must be able to shake off any feelings of condemnation, and if you cannot, you will have no confidence before God. Without confidence, your faith will not work, and without faith, you cannot please God or receive from Him the things you need in order to do the things He has called you to do (I Corinthians 4:4; Hebrews 10:22, 11:6).

It was love that called you and separated you and gave you Jesus, who shed His blood for you and wiped your sin off the face of heaven and earth. When you begin to walk and become a good steward of the commandment of love, this is when you need to take your God-given authority and dominion over the land, and possess it in love. When you walk in love, you are walking blameless in His presence (II Corinthians 5:18-20).

You know you are Christ's ambassador! Just as you were reconciled to God through Jesus, He now entrusts you to tell others that they, too, can have a personal relationship with Him. Think of someone to whom you can be Christ's ambassador, and pray for an opportunity to share God's love with that person.

I am going to say it again: When you mess things up and get off the right track with God, don't run and hide from Him, but run to Him; run to His open arms and ask forgiveness for your sin knowing, "If we confess our sins, he is faithful and just to forgive us our sins, and to cleanse us from all unrighteousness." The key here is the fact that He, Jesus, is faithful and just, faithful and just to forgive us our sins, faithful and just to cleanse us from all unrighteousness. And He will do it when you exercise your faith; believing that He is faithful and righteous and confess your sin before Him.

A PRAYER FOR REPENTANCE AND CLEANSING.

Father, I praise You and thank You for the glorious gift of Your love that covers me with the precious blood of Jesus, and for its power to forgive and cleanse me. I ask You to shine the light of Your love into my heart by Your Holy Spirit and show me any part of me that is anything less than the expression of Your love. Anything that keeps me from loving You with all my heart, and all my soul and all my might. Anything that keeps me from loving my neighbor and anything that keeps me from loving myself. (Now give the Holy Spirit a moment to show you any violation of the law of love in your life).

I now judge myself according to I Corinthians 11:31-32, and I confess the unloving way in me of <u>name the problem</u>. I repent of it and I believe Your Word that, as I have confessed my sins, You are faithful and just to forgive my sin and to cleanse me of all that is not right, all unrighteousness. I trust You to keep me right and just—like You saved me, by the power of Jesus' blood.

I yield myself to Your Spirit that is within me to keep my spirit system clean and to keep my conscience clear and to keep me from falling back into my previous condition or worse. And I stand firm that my clean spirit system will be a vessel for Your overflow into my life and into the lives of everyone in my world. In Jesus' Name.

Now start walking in the Light. Your mind, your body, and your feelings may still have the symptoms of the sin, and the devil will try to pull you back into your old feelings, especially when you come into contact with other people who are not walking in "the light of life" (John 8:12). Remember what Jesus has done for you.

> I, even I, am he that blotteth out thy transgressions for mine own sake, and will not remember thy sins.
> Put me in remembrance: let us plead together; declare thou, that thou mayest be justified (Isaiah 43:25-26; Jeremiah 31:34).

Regardless of what you may have done, you need a deeper revelation of God, and what He means when he says in Jeremiah 31:34, "I will remember your sins no more." Once you have confessed your sins and asked God for forgiveness, if you continue to bring them up to Him every time you go to Him in prayer, you are reminding Him of something He has promised to forget. Once you have confessed your sins to God and have asked Him to forgive you of them, He has not only forgiven you, but He has actually forgotten them. Whatever your sin or failure, you need to confess it to God and then let it go. Stop punishing yourself for something in the past. Refuse to remember something God has chosen to forget.

You are a child of the most-high God. He has breathed His very life into you, and you have His royal blood flowing in your veins. God saw you before you were ever formed in your mother's womb. He knew you and planned out your life before you were born. You are a person of divine destiny. You have a God-given assignment here on this earth, something you can accomplish that no one else can. You are an original and God has accepted and approved of you.

No mater how bad you mess things up, you have a right to come boldly before God's throne of grace (Hebrews 4:16) and regain your place as a favored son. It is so important that I am going to say it one more time: when you mess up, never, never run from God and hide, but run to Him. You still have your crown of favor and your robe of righteousness. Wear them and be proud!

Don't let what has happened in the past contaminate your thinking with the lies of the devil, but call things that are not as though they were (Romans 4:17). Stop dwelling on the negative lies and start dwelling on the positive things God says about you; and start speaking positive words of faith over your life, and develop a new self image of who you are in Christ.

Such as; "I am a born again, spirit filled, holy, righteous, justified son of Almighty God. I am a new creature, created in Christ Jesus, my old sin nature has passed away, and all things have become new. I am the apple of God's eye, I have a future and a destiny and I know that good things are in store for me. I am blessed, I am anointed, I am valuable, I am talented, I am creative, I walk in the favor of God and the comfort of the Holy Ghost, and whatever I touch will prosper and succeed. I am strong in the Lord and the power of His might and I am well able to do what God has called me to do."

When you start talking like that, acting like that, walking like that, and thinking like that, you will allow God to enter in and cause it to come to pass (Mark 11:23).

> For, as we all know, He [Christ] did not take hold of angels [the fallen angels, to give them a helping and delivering hand], but He did take hold of [the fallen] descendants of Abraham [to reach out to them a helping and delivering hand].
>
> So it is evident that it was essential that He be made like His brethren in every respect, in order that He might become a merciful (sympathetic) and faithful High Priest in the things related to God, to make atonement and propitiation for the people's sins.
>
> For because He Himself [in His humanity] has suffered in being tempted (tested and tried), He is able [immediately] to run to the cry of (assist, relieve) those who are being tempted and tested and tried [and who therefore are being exposed to suffering] (Hebrews 2:16-18 AMP).

> It's obvious, of course, that he didn't go to all this trouble for angels. It was for people like us, children of Abraham.
>
> That's why he had to enter into every detail of human life. Then, when he came before God as high priest to get rid of the people's sins.
>
> He would have already experienced it all himself—all the pain, all the testing—and would be able to help where help was needed (Hebrews 2:16-18 The Message Bible).

Here we see Jesus as a merciful and faithful High Priest who is standing between God and all Christians. So for Him to be faithful to God He has to be merciful and faithful to us.

There is no way, because God cannot lie, that you can go in faith before God standing on the Word of God, making a requirement of the High Priestly ministry of Jesus, for Him to refuse your request. God is faithful, and for Him to refuse would be unfaithful (Titus 1:2; Psalm 91:14-6).

> If we confess our sins, he is faithful and just [righteous] to
> forgive us our sins, and to cleanse us from all unrighteousness
> (I John 1:9).

Think of the word "justice." Justice is the right thing to do. If you are receiving justice, all things are supposed to come out right. This word "just" here is used in the King James translation for the word righteous. To be righteous is to be reconciled to right standing with God. Righteousness is a covenant word meaning; being made right, or to be reconciled to right standing with God. Righteousness is a covenant word and in I John 1:9 it simply means your sins have been blotted out or removed. Jesus is not only faithful, but He is righteous to forgive us our sin and to cleanse us from all unrighteousness.

This is not talking specifically to the sinner in the world but to born-again Christian people who have missed it, those who have gotten off of the Word and allowed sin into their lives. It is specifically talking about those who have violated the commandment of love.

If you keep the commandment of love, sin will no longer be a problem in your life. If you continue your walk with God and are a good steward of the commandment to love God and your neighbor, your love for God and your fellow man will be in your memory all of the time, because love covers a multitude of sins. Walking in love will eliminate the sin problem from your life, because sin is born out of fear, and perfected love casts out fear.

Partaking in the High Priest ministry of Jesus is the process for you to walk in a sin free (sinless) life. You do it by allowing the two words, Jesus is *faithful* and *righteous* to forgive you and cleanse you from all unrighteousness when you confess your sins by faith, not by your feelings. You cannot gauge what God has done for you by your guilt feelings. You can receive your forgiveness and have your spirit totally cleansed of all unrighteousness and still have symptoms of sin and guilt from it in your mind and in your body, particularly if it was there any length of time.

This is why I keep telling you when you sin, to run to Jesus, not from him. When you sin, stop, and get it out of there and do not allow any roots to get started. Jesus is not just faithful and just but a merciful High Priest. Get to know Him, and know you never have to be afraid of Him or afraid to come to Him. He is faithful and right and will never hurt you.

Be especially careful to not allow unforgivness to get into you and allow it to take root. It will manifest itself in you as bitterness, and it will choke the flow of God in your life and cause trouble and bitter torment (Hebrews 12:15). You simply cannot afford that.

> There is therefore now no condemnation to them which are in Christ Jesus, who walk not after the flesh, but after the Spirit.
> For the law of the Spirit of life in Christ Jesus hath made me free from the law of sin and death (Romans 8:1-2).

A law is something that works the same way every time it is put to work according to instructions. Spiritual law works every time it is applied correctly. God never does anything without saying it first. By working the spiritual laws of manifestation, heaven releases the recourses on earth to those who belong to Him.

You can contaminate a law and it will work in different ways or it will not work at all. Fear contaminates faith. Fear tolerated is faith contaminated. If you operate by the law of God, it will work for you 100% of the time, and it will work for anybody who will allow it to.

Verse 1 tells us, therefore there is now no condemnation to me if I walk after the spirit or if I walk after that law of the Spirit of life, instead of my flesh. I know that I cannot go by what my flesh is telling me. I cannot determine whether I have been forgiven or not by what my flesh or my feelings tell me or by what someone has said to me. I know I have to go by the faithfulness and the exactness and the mercifulness of Jesus my High Priest. And I know He will do exactly what He said He would do, because I am doing what He has told me to do. He has instructed me to confess the sin and believe that I receive when I pray. And by doing this I have put the law of the spirit of life in Christ Jesus into operation. This is what He is High Priest over. He is Lord over the law of sin and death; so that law has no authority over you and me because we are in Christ Jesus. The law of the spirit of life is in Christ Jesus. It is in His name, it is in His Word, it is in His life, it is in His anointing, it is in Him, and it is in you and me because we are complete in Him (Colossians 2:10).

Don't let the devil drag you back down. Tell him: God has forgiven you of all your sin, you are redeemed by the blood of Jesus; you have been made the righteousness of God in Christ Jesus and He has made you worthy to sit beside Him at His right hand (II Corinthians 5:21; Ephesians 2:6; Colossians 2:13).

When negative thoughts come your way, instead of dwelling on them and letting them take root, you must turn it around and get on the offensive and start declaring what God says about you. Speaking words of faith over your life is the best way to get rid of negative thoughts and form new positive ones. God's words always supersede man's words. It is the words you speak which guide your life in the direction you desire it to go.

Your mind should be full of positive thoughts about how God thinks about you. God dosen't make trash—you are His best, you are good, you are not defective, you are not a mistake, you have worth, you have value and no matter what comes against you, you are a victor not a victim. You are a child of the Most High God. God has breathed His very life into you. You have His royal blood flowing in your veins (Genesis 2:7; Jeremiah 1:5, 29:11).

You have the God-given ability to stop negative thoughts and replace them with positive thoughts by speaking out what God has said about you. And when you speak those positive things aloud, your faith in God and the things of God will be increased. You only need to speak loud enough for you to hear what you are saying, because Romans 10:17 tells us "faith comes by hearing the Word of God."

Words are like seeds. When you speak them out and hear them, they take root and the crop they produce depends on whether you water them by continually thinking about them and fertilizing them with either positive or negative words. It is what you do with them that counts. You have the final say and nobody but you can keep you from doing what God has called you to do.

Don't let other people or circumstances keep you from fulfilling your destiny. It's not up to them, it is up to you! You are the only one who will keep you from being what God has created you to be.

Remember, God is proud of you, He said you can do all things through Christ (Philippians 4:13). He says your best days are not behind you but are in front of you. Get in agreement with God and declare you are blessed, valuable, and that you have a bright future.

You are the one in control of what you see with your eyes and hear with your ears. You are responsible for what gets into your heart—for what you believe. Put your eyes and ears on the Word of God, receive it and believe it. This is how your faith will come to you.

Once you begin to place your focus on the Word, faith develops within your spirit. Faith in the Word becomes the first response in your heart when challenges come. Your faith is activated when you speak words that rise up from your heart, and are in agreement with God's Word. It is then that good things will happen! (Matthew 12:34).

Examine and test and evaluate your own selves to see whether you are holding to your faith and showing the proper fruits of it. Test and prove yourselves [not Christ.] (II Corinthians 13:5 AMP).

Start taking notice of what you are saying, looking at, and what you are hearing; and if you will stay in faith and get rid of the negative, harmful thoughts, God will take what the devil meant for your harm and turn it around for your good and use it to your advantage!

Jesus is offering you His mind cleansed of all your sins. Now fill His mind with what you want Him to remember about you, positive, faith filled words, not with how badly you feel or how unworthy you are. Fill His mind and yours with words of faith and redemption. With scriptures that declare just who you are in Christ, with verses loaded with God's grace and mercy, love and goodness (I Corinthians 2:16).

To release God's plan in your life, you must stop mentally living in the past. You must begin to think in agreement with God, and once you do, you can begin to speak in agreement with Him. By doing so you can actually prophesy your own future.

Example: Greater is He that is in me, than he that is in the world. I am strengthened from within, because the greater one within me is the power of God and the wisdom of God. I am strong in the Lord and the power of His might. I am moving free in His strength and in His power. I've learned how to put the Christ in me to work for me. I have, dwelling in me, the Spirit of God, who raised Jesus from the dead! I have God's wisdom, strength, and ability in me, and I'm daring to think God's thoughts. I'm learning how to let that wisdom govern my intellect, and I'm letting God speak through me, because I have the mind of Christ. He is the strength of my life, so whom shall I fear? God in me has made me greater than my enemies. God has enabled me to put my heel on the neck of weakness, fear, and inability. I stand and declare that whosoever believeth in Him shall not be put to shame. Therefore, I cannot be put to shame, because I walk in the grace and favor of the greater one who lives inside of me.

Don't ever think that you have got to get yourself into a position where God will accept you. He will take you just the way you are right now. There is only one sin so great that He will not forgive you.

> All manner of sin and blasphemy shall be forgiven unto men: but the blasphemy against the Holy Ghost shall not be forgiven unto men (Matthew 12:31).

17

FEAR THAT IS TOLERATED IS FAITH CONTAMINATED

For God hath not given us the spirit of fear, but of power,
and of love, and of a sound mind (II Timothy 1:7).

Fear, power, love, and a sound mind are all spiritual forces. The spirit of
fear, the spirit of power, the spirit of love, and a sound mind are all different
things. The forces of power, love, and a sound mind come from God but the
spirit of fear does not come from God. Fear is the direct opposite from faith.

The spirits of power, love, and a sound mind are connected to the law of
the spirit of life in Christ Jesus, as found in Romans 8:2, and the spirit of fear
is connected to the law of sin and death. A mind that is under the influence
of the spirit of fear is not connected to nor is it associated with a sound mind.
We can see this separation in I John 4:18. "There is no fear in love; but
perfect love casteth out fear; because fear hath torment. He that feareth is not
made perfect in love" (II Timothy 1:7).

Notice fear hath torment, and the spirit of fear is the tormentor. Jesus
dealt with the tormenter in demon-possessed people in Matthew 4:24. So
we can see that the fear in one's life is connected to the spirit of fear, and that
your faith connects you to the spirit of love.

Do you recognize fear's presence in your everyday life? Worry is a
manifestation of fear, negative thinking is an expression of fear, and struggling
to believe God's Word is a serious sign of fear's presence in your life. Depression
is a manifestation of fear and grief, and all forms of loss are fear's calling cards.
Being frightened is only a small part of fear. Fear is planted in your heart
through the words you hear and things you see. Unless God's love is working

in your life casting fear out, fear is working continually to connect and open up your heart to the spirit of fear.

Worry is faith in fear or a manifestation of fear, and negative thinking is an expression of fear. Worry is the inability to forget the troubles that will never happen, and fear is simply "false evidence that appears real." Fear is having more faith in what the devil is telling you than what God is telling you.

Fear's job is to hinder, harass, trouble, and try to stop the anointing of God any way it can. Fear is designed to get you to think what God has promised in His Word will not come to pass in your life. This is the ultimate goal and objective of the spirit of fear (Romans 4:21).

"Fear not" is a command (Luke 12:32). To continue in fear stops God's blessings from coming on your life; and that's sin. Crying about it won't stop it. Being mad at yourself or others won't stop it. The simple solution is to repent according to I John 1:9. "If we confess our sins, he is faithful and just to forgive us our sins, and to cleanse us from all unrighteousness." Be quick to repent. Do not try to hide anything from God. God will never reject you. He knows everything anyway. Confess your sins and allow the blood of Jesus to cleanse you from all unrighteousness on a regular basis. I John 4:18 tells us God's love will move fear out of our lives. "There is no fear in love; but perfect love casteth out fear: because <u>fear hath torment</u>. He that feareth is not made perfect in love."

Take time to judge yourself by the Word of God, use the 10 commandments; I Corinthians 13:4-8 and I John 2:15-16 as a guideline. "For if we judge ourselves, we should not be judged" (I Corinthians 11:31). We are supposed to judge ourselves to ensure we are living in line with the Word of God but we are not to judge others. Matthew 7:1-2 (AMP) says, "Do not judge and criticize and condemn others, so that you may not be judged and criticized and condemned, and in accordance with the measure you [use to] deal out to others, it will be dealt out again to you."

Judging yourself is not easy; however, it is necessary. It's hard to be critical of others when you're judging yourself. I am not talking about self-condemnation. To judge yourself is to look honestly at yourself in the light of the Word of God, not in the shadow of hiding things you know should be separated from your life. Be blunt with yourself, be strong. Stand up and face your problems whatever they are. Call it sin! Say it aloud and don't be afraid of what God might do. He has known about it all along. If you find yourself being judgmental or ungrateful at times, simply change the way you are thinking about the situation and repent. Put your thoughts, words, and actions into line with God's Word, and develop a grateful heart. Ask yourself, am I doing what God has asked me to do? Am I doing all that I can and know to do to the best of my God given ability? Do I love others as God loves me? Don't condemn yourself, because the things we hide in darkness are the things which have power over us. For "There is nothing hid that will not be manifested; neither was anything kept secret, but that it should come abroad" (Mark 4:22).

Are you allowing the spirit of fear to dominate your life? If you are, repent and confess your sin and move on with God. Fear is a demonic force and is not from God. Fear connects you to the spirit of death (II Timothy 1:7). Timidity, which is the same as fear, is not from God, but God has given us power and love, a calm and well-balanced mind, discipline, and self-control. We are not cowards because we feel fear, but we are when we let fear control our decisions. Fear is a spirit that produces physical and emotional stress. The Word says many times, "fear not." The way to conquer fear is to confess the Word of God concerning your situation, press on through it, and get to the other side, the side of freedom, which is the side of power.

The second you realize that the spirit of fear is trying to move into your life again, start quoting scripture to the devil and he will flee. Remember, the Word says, "Submit yourselves therefore to God, resist the devil and he will flee [as if in terror] from you" (James 4:7).

You submit yourself to God by allowing the Holy Spirit to be the dominate force in your life, your leader and your guide; by reading and meditating on His Word. And you resist the devil by acting in faith, exercising your authority by quoting the Word of God to him.

If you want your prayers answered, be sure you are submitted unto God. It is very difficult for God to answer someone's prayers when they are prideful. You must be submitted to God, to His Word, doing things His way, not the world's way. To resist: means to stand firm against, to withstand. The battleground is in your mind. That is where the devil will meet you every time. Ephesians 6:11-18 (AMP) tells us to take the whole amour of God. That amour is God's Word which has been planted into our hearts.

> Put on God's whole armor [the armor of a heavy-armed soldier which God supplies], that you may be able successfully to stand up against [all] the strategies and deceits of the devil.

For we are not wrestling with flesh and blood [contending only with physical opponents], but against the despotisms, against this present darkness, against the spirit forces of wickedness in the heavenly (supernatural sphere).

Therefore put on God's complete armor, that you may be able to resist and stand your ground on the evil day [of danger], and having done all [the crisis demands], to stand [firmly in your place].

Stand therefore [hold your ground], having tightened the belt of truth around your loins and having put on the breastplate of integrity and of moral rectitude and right standing with God.

And having shod your feet in preparation [to face the enemy with the firm-footed stability, the promptness, and the readiness produced by the good news] of the gospel of peace.

Lift up over all the [covering] shield of saving faith, upon which you can quench all the flaming missiles of the wicked [one].

And take the helmet of salvation and the sword that the Spirit wields, which is the Word of God.

Pray at all times (on every occasion, in every season) in the Spirit, with all [manner of] prayer and entreaty. To that end keep alert and watch with strong purpose perseverance, interceding in behalf of all the saints (God's consecrated people) (Ephesians 6:11-18 AMP).

When the devil shows up, send God's Word that has been planted into your heart out to defeat him. God's words are your weapons. You resist the devil with the Word of God coming out of your mouth. You have to open up your mouth and overcome those thoughts with words. Thoughts will not overcome thoughts, but words will overcome thoughts. So when a negative thought shows up, you must open up your mouth and stop that negative thought with the Word of God. And the Word of God will capture that negative thought and it will cast it down and then you can make your mind obey the Word of God.

Get a confession book of God's promises which are available at almost every Christian book store and read the verses that pertain to the area in which the negative thoughts cover. An excellent web sight to use is: Uversion. com. Read the verses over and over until those thoughts are removed from your thinking. Just refuse to allow those thoughts to occupy your mind.

When you do your part, the devil will flee from you as if in fear. The word "flee" means to run with fear. He just hates it when you confess God's Word and he especially hates it when you confess the Name of Jesus.

> That at the name of Jesus every knee should bow, of things in heaven, and things in earth, and things under the earth; And that every tongue should confess that Jesus Christ is Lord, to the glory of God the Father (Philippians 2:10-11).

The devil always shows up with fear trying to get you to fear but when you resist him with the Word of God and the name of Jesus, he will run with the fear he showed up with.

Satan is helpless against you when you know you have been delivered from his control. I John 2:14 states, ". . . ye are strong, and the Word of God abideth in you, and ye have overcome the wicked one."

No matter what comes against you, it will not succeed if you stand in the authority Jesus has conferred upon you. Luke 10:19 states, "Behold, I give unto you power (authority) to tread on serpents and scorpions and over all the power of the enemy, and nothing shall by any means hurt you." Jesus has shattered Satan's power over you and you should never fear him again. It's time for you to begin acting as if you truly believe this, and when you do, "you cannot be defeated."

Trials and adversities will come your way, but they cannot keep you from living a victorious life. Psalms 34:19 (AMP) states, "Many evils confront the [consistently] righteous, but the Lord delivers him out of them all." But you have to allow Him to do it by confessing the Word of God which applies to that situation!

God never intended for you to fail, and nothing makes Him happier than to see you overcoming everything Satan throws your way.

If you are facing adversity, just refuse to give up. For with God on your side, you cannot be defeated! You may feel as if you can't take anymore, but if you'll refuse to give up, then God will make a way. II Corinthians 1:10 (AMP) states, "[for it is he] who rescued and saved us . . . He will again deliver us [from danger and destruction and draw us to Himself]." God turns Satan's setbacks into your victories; you may be struck down, but you are never struck out and destroyed when you refuse to give up. The Word tells us we are beyond defeat when you know this and act upon it, and Satan cannot keep you from overcoming all of his attacks against you. Satan is not all-powerful as he would have you believe. You are the one with the power (authority), but it does you little good if you refuse to use it. Luke 24:49 states you are "endued with power from on high:" Endued, means to put on and to be clothed with. This means you have to wear your power and authority like you would a coat. It also means to be skilled. This indicates you should practice using your power and authority and not let it lay dormant.

If Satan is prevailing over you and defeating you, then it has to be for one of the following reasons:

1. A lack of knowledge of your authority over him.
2. Knowing your authority but failing to act upon it.
3. Knowing and using your authority but giving up too quickly because you've become deceived into thinking you cannot win. The devil will test you with everything he has at his disposal, but you are stronger "in Christ" than he is.

Defeat is not in God's plan for your life. Deuteronomy 28:13 says, "And the Lord will make thee the head, and not the tail; and thou shall be above only, and thou shalt not be beneath." So you must be careful to never leave an open door for the devil to get in!

> We love him, because he first loved us.
> If a man say, I love God, and hateth his brother, he is a liar: for he that loveth not his brother whom he hath seen, how can he love God whom he hath not seen?
> And this commandment have we from him, That he who loveth God loves his brother also (I John 4:19-21).

The minute you start hating people, you give the devil access to your heart—your innermost sanctuary. And once he's in there, he messes everything up. He disrupts your communication and fellowship with the Lord. He brings in all kinds of turmoil and fear. As James 3:16 says, "Where strife is, there is confusion and every evil work." It doesn't always have anything to do with what was said or what was done to you; it has everything to do with what you said, or how you reacted to the other person. Choose your words carefully, because you will have to account for the idle, thoughtless things you say (Matthew 12:36-37). Words are seeds; they are containers for power. They carry creative or destructive power, and they can produce a good harvest or a bad harvest in your life and in the lives of your loved ones. Matthew 12:31 says "By your words you will be justified, and by thy words thou shall be condemned." It has to do with how you react (Proverbs 18:21).

Every word we speak can be a brick to build with or a bulldozer to destroy. Romans 8:2 tells us, "The law of the spirit of life in Christ Jesus has made you free from the law of sin and death." But if you activate the law of sin and death it suddenly has authority over you and it will come on you because—"it shall come to pass" (Deuteronomy 28:15).

Sin separates the Spirit of God from man, and without the Spirit of God working in you, you are under the Law of sin and death (Romans 8:2).

Colossians 1:27 (AMP) says, "Christ within and among you the Hope of [realizing the] glory." That Glory is the manifest presence of God in your life, that glory is God's anointing, and this means that God's glory and God's love is revealed "through you!" God has chosen to reveal His love and His glory to others through the story of your life. Through your life, the cycle of love is intended to start over in someone else's life, again and again and again (II Corinthians 3:2).

The Bible tells us that Christ within and among us is the Hope of glory (Colossians 1:27). We can realize and experience the glory of God in our lives because Christ is in us. He is our hope of seeing better things. The glory of God is His manifested excellence. As a child of God, we have a blood-bought right to experience the best that God has planned for us. Much of the time we feel defeated as we look at ourselves and our lack of ability. What we need to do is remember that Christ in us is our Hope. God is looking for someone who will believe and receive, so start expecting more of His glory in your life. He is waiting to manifest His glory to you and though you. Remember, I John 4:21 tells us, "And this commandment we have from him, that he who loveth God loves his brother."

Your life is the only Bible some people will ever read. As Christians, people watch us and occasionally put us to the test. Always be on guard, and remember that you carry the name of Jesus Christ on your shoulders when you call yourself a "Christian." People see more than they hear. Live your life so that others can see it is Christ who lives in you. Don't live in crisis, live in Christ. Let others see you are a person who lets Christ—the hope of glory—rule and reign in you. What are people seeing when they look at you? Once you begin to grasp this concept, you will be able to love not just out of obedience but with real affection and depth, because you will realize God has created you first to receive love and then to give it away. And when you give it away, you will see breakthroughs in ways you never imagined.

Love is the most powerful component and the number-one priority of the Christian life. It is only by walking in love that we truly come to know and have an intimate relationship with God. I John 4:7 tells us, "Beloved, let us love one another: for love is of God; and every one that loveth is born of God, and knoweth God. He that loveth not knoweth not God; for God is love."

Don't try to be a Christian in the flesh but, "put on charity [love], which is the bond of perfectness. And let the peace of God rule in your hearts, to which also you are called in one body; and be ye thankful" (I John 4:14-15). The world is looking for something real, something tangible. People are looking for love, and God is love, and God dwells in us. We know God has the answers to the searching hearts of those around us, and He will meet the needs of the people we encounter in our daily lives if we will simply reach out to them in faith.

Everything God does here on earth is done by the principle of seed time and harvest. To start, you must plant or sow the first love seed. The seed does not develop overnight, or through your effort to love your ugly neighbor. That is not the place to start. Where you start is by loving God, by simply saying "I love you, Father and I receive Your love for me today." When you do, the Holy Ghost, the Spirit of Love, will start knocking down the old walls and stretch you on the inside so that you will start learning things you didn't think you could learn. What you plant today is what you will reap tomorrow! A crop is raised by tilling the ground, planting the seed, watering and fertilizing that seed, and keeping the weeds out until it has matured and then it is harvested.

When Jesus gave the great love commandments, He gave them in order, a first and a second commandment. In Matthew 22:37-39, He said, "Thou shalt love the Lord thy God with all thy heart, and with all thy soul, and with all thy mind. This is the first and great commandment. And the second is like unto it, Thou shalt love thy neighbour as thyself."

You won't become efficient overnight, but you have to start somewhere, and you have the Holy Spirit in you to help you carry it out, To start, just let the Word of Christ dwell in you richly, in all wisdom, and let the Holy Spirit help you imitate God (Colossians 3:16). If you let the Word of God have its home in your heart and mind, it will give you insight to intelligence and wisdom; so let God's rich Word dwell in you, and you will see a difference in your life!

Just like falling in love with a person, falling in love with God takes time, focus, and commitment. There are several ways to practice the presence of God and deepen your love relationship with Him, but I believe the simplest way is by realizing and believing just how much He loves you (I John 4:19). Just take Him at His Word. Fall in love with Him; and let Him woo you, or let Him court you (Hosea 2:14). Let Him speak great and amazing things over you, things that may seem too great or too amazing. But believe them, because everything God says is fact; these things will happen. If you ever ask God what He thinks of you, His answer will coincide with Jeremiah 29:11 and I Corinthians 2:9. "For I know the thoughts that I think toward you thoughts of peace and not of evil, to give you a future and a hope." And, "Eye hath not seen, nor ear heard, neither have entered into the heart of man the things which God hath prepared for them that love him." God loves you that much!

God has you on His mind and wants you to have "the good life.

> For we are God's [own] handiwork (His workmanship), recreated in Christ Jesus, [born anew] that we may do those good works which God predestined (planned beforehand) for us [taking paths which He prepared ahead of time], that we should walk in them [living the good life which He prearranged and made ready for us to live] (Ephesians 2:10 AMP).

God is a good God, and He wants the best for you, just like most parents want the best for their children. James 1:17 (AMP) tells us, "Every good and every perfect (free, large, full) gift is from above; it comes down from the Father of all [that gives] light, in [the shinning of] Whom there can be no variation [rising or setting] or shadow cast by His turning [as in an eclipse]."

None of us are perfect, and we all make mistakes. Remember, when you do sin you need to run back into God's arms not away from Him. Anytime you stumble and fall into sin, when you go to God in repentance, He will always forgive you—no matter how big or small the transgression. The devil will try to put you under condemnation, but you have only to resist the devil and he will flee from you. When the devil reminds you of the mistakes you have made, just take a little time and remind him of some of the mistakes he has made. You might also remind him of his destiny, and that the last page of the Bible says, "we win!"

Remember, as a born-again son of God, you are walking in the benefits of a blood covenant from the Cross that says your sins are totally forgiven, never to be remembered against you. You are adopted into the royal family of God and are no more a servant, but a son; and if a son, then an heir of God through Christ. So don't ever let the devil tell you that you aren't good enough! (Ephesians 1:7; Isaiah 43:25; John 1:12; Galatians 4:7).

The Word of God is like a mirror, and when you look into it, you won't see yourself the way the devil says you are but the way God says you are. God doesn't see failures and sin; He sees the blood of Jesus.

When you look in the mirror of God's Word, you will see yourself the way your heavenly Father sees you. He sees you healed, without sickness. He sees you free, without bondage. He sees you full of joy, not sorrow, and He sees you a winner, not a loser, because apart from Him you can do nothing.

Always remember, boldness is a fearless confidence in God—confidence in yourself and in your life. You start by getting into God's Word until you are fully persuaded that what God has promised to you in His Word He is able to perform or deliver (Romans 4:21).

Peter tells us in I Peter 2:2 to desire the sincere milk of the Word so we will grow. So take time to read the Word and find out who you are "in Christ." This is how you will move beyond your carnal, fleshy nature. The Word of God teaches us there is a similarity between spiritual growth and physical growth. The more you read the Word and fellowship with the Lord through prayer and meditation, the easier it will be to bring your carnal, fleshy nature into subjection. Remember, your past is gone, and you are a new creature in Christ, so look beyond where you are and see with the eyes of faith, believing God for even the impossible! It costs nothing to be positive and believe that God can change you and your life. Start your blessings by confessing that you love your life, and be thankful in all things, no matter what the circumstances you may be in.

Jesus tells us in Matthew 23:12; Luke 14:11, 18:14, "those who exalt themselves will be brought down," and Peter instructs us in I Peter 5:6, to, "Humble yourselves therefore under the mighty hand of God that he may exalt you in due time." Change takes place when you're thankful and not critical. Do not complain, your situation may not look all that good, but don't complain about it. I Thessalonians 5:18 (AMP) says, "Thank [God] in everything [no matter what the circumstances may be, be thankful and give thanks], for this is the will of God for you [who are] in Christ Jesus [the Revealer and Mediator of that will.]" (Colossians 2:7).

If you want God's best, you must do God's Word. In order to receive God's promises, you must first believe they are yours through Christ Jesus. Ephesians 1:20 tells us God "raised him (Jesus) from the dead, and set him at his own right hand in the heavenly places." And in Ephesians 2:6 tells us God "raised us up together, and made us sit together in heavenly places in Christ Jesus." If we are seated with Christ, and Christ is seated next to God the Father in heaven, then, spiritually speaking, we are also seated next to God the Father in heaven. And if God raised Jesus "far above all principality, and power, and might, and dominion, and every name that is named, not only in this world, but also in that which is to come: And hath put all things under his feet, and gave him to be the head over all things to the church" (Ephesians 1:21-22). This means that whatever Jesus received from the Father becomes yours as well and all you have to do is believe it and receive it by faith (II Timothy 3:15-17; Mark 11:24; Colossians 2:12)!

The Bible depicts Jesus after His resurrection as seated in heavenly places at the right hand of God. Being "seated" refers to being in the rest of God. God wants each of us to enter His rest and our part is to believe and rest in Him, and His part is to work on our behalf. Physically we are on the earth, but simultaneously we can be spiritually seated with Him in heaven.

I encourage you to be assured in your faith that God will follow through with what He has promised you in His Word. Get His promises into your mind and think about them; speak of them; and let your faith increase (Hebrews 4:9-11).

You will find no greater joy in life than helping someone find the unconditional love and the unending hope which comes only through a lasting relationship with Jesus Christ. Make it your goal in life to do those things that please God (John 8:29). Live the life God has intended for you, a complete life of joy, fulfillment, and fruitful living. Don't settle for anything less than God's best. Job 5:9 (The Message Bible) says "He's famous for great and unexpected acts; there's no end to His surprises."

18

PRAYING FOR OTHERS

First of all, then, I admonish and urge that petitions, prayers, intercessions, and thanksgivings be offered on behalf of all men.

For kings [our president] and all who are in positions of authority or high responsibility, that [outwardly] we may pass a quiet and undisturbed life [and inwardly] a peaceable one in all godliness and reverence and seriousness in every way.

For such [praying] is good and right, and [it is] pleasing and acceptable to God our Savior.

Who wishes all men to be saved and [increasingly] to perceive and recognize and discern and know precisely and correctly the [divine] Truth [the Word of God] (I Timothy 2:1-4 AMP).

As a born-again son of God, you are alive unto God and have been empowered by His Spirit to take your place and use the name of Jesus to stand against the forces of evil to prevent them from moving in and taking over.

As you stand in the gap and take up the hedge of protection over those who you are praying for, the conditions you are seeing will be turned around, and the blessings of God will flow into their lives. You will also see the Kingdom Of God enhanced, and the Church of Our Lord Jesus Christ multiplied in number and gain momentum. And as you do this, men will see your light shine as the truth of God's Word goes forth in great power with the Holy Ghost in manifestation.

There are many people out there who have chosen not to follow Jesus Christ and make Him their Lord and Savior—many because they have never heard the Gospel preached, some who have allowed Satan (the god of this world) to blind their minds so they cannot see "the light of the gospel of the glory of Christ," but many who have simply decided to make Satan their spiritual leader (II Corinthians 4:3-4).

Everyone either serves God or Satan; if you don't choose to make the decision, it will be made for you. The satanic side of spiritual warfare is carried out by demonic spirits and those people they controls. He cannot do it by himself. He must find a person or persons that he can possess and through them accomplish his evil works.

You cannot interfere with another person's will, but you can literally play hell with those demonic spirits which are influencing his or her life. There is no prayer you can pray that will change the will of another human being, although a prayer of intercession can interfere with the demonic forces that are influencing him or her and allow that person to see the light shining in the darkness.

You can also change the circumstances which surround that person with your prayers and help create situations that will bring said person into contact with the Lord. Jesus instructed us to "pray ye therefore the Lord of the harvest, that he would send forth laborers into His harvest (Luke 10:2)." You just need to ask God to send born-again, spirit-filled, holy, righteous, justified, Word-believing, people across the paths of those whom you are praying for.

You have the authority to interfere with the assignments of those evil spirits (Luke 10:19: ". . . the god of this world that hath blinded the minds of them which believe not, least the light of the glorious gospel of Christ, who is the image of God, should shine unto them" (II Corinthians 4:4). We do not have control over human wills, but we do have control over evil spirits that bind and blind men.

Remember, "We wrestle not against flesh and blood, but against principalities, against powers, against the rulers of the darkness of this world, against spiritual wickedness in high places" (Ephesians 6:12). The devils and demon spirits can only do what you allow them to do because you are told in Colossians 2:10, ". . . you are complete in Him [in Christ], which is the head of all principality and power," and Ephesians 1:3 tells us, ". . . you have been blessed with all spiritual blessings in heavenly places in Christ." Remember, God has also given you authority to trample on, "serpents and scorpions and over all the power of the enemy" (Luke10:19). It is your responsibility to take authority over those unseen forces and bind them from operating openly.

God Himself is the Power, the Force, behind this authority. You and I, as believers, when we are fully conscious of this divine authority, we can therefore face the enemy without fear or hesitation. For behind the authority possessed by us, the believer is a power far greater than the power that backs the Devil and his crowd. And they are compelled to recognize that authority!

So now you can clean your house and be rid of those demonic spirits that are oppressing you and your family! You have the fullness of the Godhead living on the inside of you and you have all the power and authority which he has delegated to you. You have the God given authority and when you act in faith based on God's Word He will back you up all the way.

And then pray the Ephesians 1:16-21 prayer for them.

> I cease not to give thanks for you, making mention of you in my prayers;
>
> That the God of our Lord Jesus Christ, the Father of glory, may give unto you the spirit of wisdom and revelation in the knowledge of him:
>
> The eyes of your understanding being enlightened; that you may know what is the hope of his calling, and what the riches of the glory of his inheritance in the saints,
>
> And what is the exceeding greatness of his power to us-ward who believe, according to the working of his mighty power,
>
> Which he wrought in Christ, when he raised him from the dead and set him at his own right hand in the heavenly places.
>
> Far above all principality and power and might and dominion, and every name that is named, not only in this age but also in that which is to come. In Jesus' Name.

Put your name or the persons name you are praying for in the space where it says "you." I encourage you to pray this prayer for yourself also so the revelation of God's Word would begin to come to you!

There was such a manifestation of the divine omnipotence of God's power in raising Jesus from the dead that it is actually the mightiest working of God! And He wants you to know what happened when this occurred. When you pray this prayer for yourself or for someone else you are asking God to give to yourself or theother person revelation knowledge of spiritual things.

Knowing what a verse says and receiving a revelation of that Word are two entirely different things. This is why it is so important to have the Holy Spirit actively working in your life.

A second prayer I encourage you to pray for yourself and others is from Ephesians 3:14-21. Stay at it, because it won't work if you pray it on a hit and miss basis. Do it morning and night, and more frequently if you can.

> For this cause I bow my knees unto the Father of our lord Jesus Christ,
>
> Of whom the whole family in heaven and earth is named,
>
> That he would grant you according to the riches of his glory, to be strengthened with might by his Spirit in your inner man;
>
> That Christ may dwell in your hearts by faith; that you being rooted and grounded in love,
>
> May be able to comprehend with all saints what is the breadth, and length, and depth, and height;
>
> And to know the love of Christ, which passeth knowledge,
>
> That you might be filled with all the fullness of God.
>
> Now unto him that is able to do exceeding abundantly above all that we ask or think, <u>according to the power that worketh in us.</u>
>
> Unto him be glory in the church by Christ Jesus throughout all ages, would without end. Amen.

My prayer for you also includes this from Colossians 1:9-11.

> I pray that you might be filled with the knowledge of his will in all wisdom and spiritual understanding;
>
> That you might walk worthy of the Lord unto all pleasing, being fruitful in every good work, and increasing in the knowledge of God.
>
> Strengthened with all might according to his glorious power unto all patience and longsuffering with joyfulness. In Jesus Name.

Pay close attention to these five verses. God is interested in your prayers, but your prayers must line up with the Word of God to be effective.

> The effective, fervent prayer of a righteous man avails much (James 5:16).

> So shall My word be that goes forth out of My mouth: it shall not return to Me void [without producing any effect, useless], but it shall accomplish that which I please and purpose, and it shall prosper in the thing for which I sent it (Isaiah 55:11 AMP).

> The earnest (heartfelt, continued) prayer of a righteousness man makes tremendous power available [dynamic in its working] (James 5:16 AMP).

> I will hasten my word to perform it (Jeremiah 1:12).

> The Lord does not delay and is not tardy or slow about what He promises, according to some people's conception of slowness, but He is long-suffering (extraordinarily patient) toward you, not desiring that any should perish, but that all should turn to repentance. (II Peter 3:9 AMP).

Be encouraged, because your time spent in prayer is never wasted. Always start or end your prayers with the Name of Jesus. When you speak His Name, you will always get God's attention (John 14:13, 15:16, and 16:23).